RESTORING THE GOSPELS' JEWISH VOICE

Studies in Judaism and Christianity

Exploration of Issues in the Contemporary Dialogue between Christians and Jews

EDITORS

Michael McGarry, CSP

Mark-David Janus, CSP, PhD

Adam Gregerman, PhD

Yehezkel Landau, DMin

Peter Pettit, PhD

Elena Procario-Foley, PhD

Ellen M. Umansky, PhD

Rabbi Stephen Wylen

A STIMULUS BOOK

Restoring the Gospels' Jewish Voice

André Chouraqui and the
Intersection of Biblical Translation
and Interfaith Dialogue

MURRAY K. WATSON

A STIMULUS BOOK

PAULIST PRESS • NEW YORK • MAHWAH, NJ

Unless otherwise indicated, the Scripture quotations contained herein are from the New Revised Standard Version: Catholic Edition, Copyright © 1989 and 1993, by the Division of Christian Education of the National Council of the Churches of Christ in the United States of America. Used by permission. All rights reserved. All translations from other non-English texts are the author's own.

Cover image of ANDRE CHOURAQUI Micheline Pelletier/Getty Images
Cover design by Sharyn Banks
Book design by Lynn Else

Copyright © 2023 by the Stimulus Foundation, Inc.

All rights reserved. No part of this publication may be reproduced, stored in a retrieval system, or transmitted in any form or by any means, electronic, mechanical, photocopying, recording, scanning, or otherwise, without either the prior written permission of the Publisher, or authorization through payment of the appropriate per-copy fee to the Copyright Clearance Center, Inc., 222 Rosewood Drive, Danvers, MA 01923, (978) 750-8400, fax (978) 646-8600, or on the Web at www.copyright.com. Requests to the Publisher for permission should be addressed to the Permissions Department, Paulist Press, 997 Macarthur Boulevard, Mahwah, NJ 07450.

Library of Congress Cataloging-in-Publication Data
Names: Watson, J. Murray, author.
Title: Restoring the gospels' Jewish voice : André Chouraqui and the intersection of biblical translation and interfaith dialogue / Murray Watson.
Description: New York ; Mahwah, NJ : Paulist Press, [2023] | Series: Studies in Judaism and Christianity | "A Stimulus Book." | Includes bibliographical references and index. | Summary: "This book is an appreciation of the life and work of André Chouraqui"—Provided by publisher.
Identifiers: LCCN 2023008838 (print) | LCCN 2023008839 (ebook) | ISBN 9780809156689 (paperback) | ISBN 9780809188291 (ebook)
Subjects: LCSH: Bible. New Testament—Criticism, interpretation, etc., Jewish. | Judaism. | Chouraqui, André, 1917–2007,
Classification: LCC BS2350 .W37 2023 (print) | LCC BS2350 (ebook) | DDC 225.6—dc23/eng/20230814
LC record available at https://lccn.loc.gov/2023008838
LC ebook record available at https://lccn.loc.gov/2023008839

ISBN 978-0-8091-5668-9 (paperback)
ISBN 978-0-8091-8829-1 (ebook)

Published by Paulist Press
997 Macarthur Boulevard
Mahwah, New Jersey 07430
www.paulistpress.com

Printed and bound in the
United States of America

There's a blaze of light in every word—
It doesn't matter which you heard,
The holy or the broken Hallelujah....

Leonard Cohen, "Hallelujah" (1984)

CONTENTS

A Chronology of André Chouraqui's Life xi

Foreword by Yehezkel Landau, DMin. xix

Acknowledgments xxvii

Preface xxix

SECTION 1:
TRANSLATION FOR TRANSFORMATION 1

Chapter 1: The Word made strange 3

    Yet another Bible translation…why?. 4

    A New Testament anew 7

    A Bible "in the language in which it was written" 8

    To adapt, or to reflect? 11

Chapter 2: Jewishness for Jesus 13

    INRI: Jesus of Nazareth, King of the Jews 14

    Chouraqui's modern-day antecedents 15

    The Jewishness of Jesus 19

Chapter 3: Enter the Hebraic matrix 24

    A mind-"altar"-ing experience. 24

    What's his name again? 25

    What's in a (place) name? Lots! 31

Contents

Chapter 4: Resurrecting moribund theological vocabulary 36
    Where's the priest? 36
    Rabbis multiplying 38
    Touched by an *angelos* 43
    Non-*prophētēs* association...........................45
    Out with the Greek, in with the Hebrew 53

Chapter 5: Cognates, formal equivalence, and the two Jerusalems 65
    Chouraqui's rendering of Hebrew dual and plural forms ...65
    Yerushalayim 66
    The Semitic linking of related verbs and nouns 69
    The future tense used as a command...................73

Chapter 6: A rich, iconoclastic legacy 77

SECTION 2:
UNE VIE TRÈS PLEINE............................... 81

Chapter 7: A man of three worlds 83
    Education both religious and secular...................90
    Chouraqui's rediscovery of Judaism 96
    The ravages of war 98
    Enduring the war and its repercussions................101
    Return to Algeria—and the start of a global career.......105
    The advent of *Nostra aetate* 109
    André and Colette: A painful parting..................110
    The promised land beckons; literary beginnings.........111

Contents

Aliyah and a new political life 113
Municipal politics in Jerusalem 117
The genesis of *La Bible Chouraqui* 121
Éminence grise 126
Mort de joie 128
Epilogue 136
Rebel translator 138
Polyglot wordsmith 139
A Jew…for Jesus 140
Afterword 143
Glossary 147
Notes 153
Bibliography 169
Index 177

A CHRONOLOGY OF ANDRÉ CHOURAQUI'S LIFE

Note: Chouraqui lived an extremely rich and event-filled life. The constraints of space mean that this chronology necessarily omits many dates that are important (arguably just as important as those included) for understanding Chouraqui's life.

His printed autobiographies, his website (https://andrechouraqui.com), and this historical website (http://www.kronobase.org/chronologie-categorie-Andr%C3%A9+Nathan+Chouraqui.html) provide timelines that are considerably more fulsome, for those who would like to explore his fascinating life in greater detail.

1917	On August 11, André Chouraqui is born in Aïn-Témouchent, Algeria, then a colony of France; a week later, he is circumcised, officially becoming part of the Jewish people.
1921	Chouraqui begins Hebrew studies at the age of four, under the local rabbi. He also begins to learn French at the kindergarten of the Salesian Sisters.
1923	Summer: An attack of childhood polio leaves Chouraqui paralyzed for several months. He learns to walk again, but his left leg is permanently weakened.
1928–34	Attends secondary school as a boarding student in Oran, a coastal city in Algeria.
1930	Summer: Celebrates his bar mitzvah at the Aïn-Témouchent synagogue.
1934	Summer: André's family arranges for him to have surgery on his leg at the La Montagne clinic in Paris, where he

	meets Christian nurse-missionaries who inspire him with their devotion to their patients—and their familiarity with the Bible.
1934–39	Studies law in Paris, graduating in 1937 with his law degree. Pursues graduate studies in law while also beginning to study Hebrew, Aramaic, and Jewish Biblical interpretation once more at the rabbinic seminary in Paris from 1937 to 1939.
1939	November: Meets Colette Boyer, who will become his first wife.
1939–40	A member of the bar in Oran (Algeria), where he practices law; Chouraqui tenders his resignation before being forced out by the racial laws of France's Vichy government.
1940	December: Colette converts to Judaism, taking the name of Sarah bat-Abraham, and she and André are married in a religious ceremony.
1941	Returns to France to pursue his studies in Judaism, first in Vichy and later in Clermont-Ferrand.

May: The Chouraquis' daughter, Emmanuèle, is born; tragically, she dies in August. |
1942	Expelled from Clermont-Ferrand with other Jews; André and Colette flee to Chaumargeais in the Haute-Loire region.
1942–45	Takes an active part in the French Resistance movement from a hiding place in south-central France; continues his Jewish studies informally and renews his friendship with Albert Camus.
1945	Returns to Paris after France's liberation, but is disillusioned and falls ill. After his recovery, he returns to

A Chronology of André Chouraqui

Algeria for further legal studies and is named a regional judge.

1947 Gravely ill, Colette returns to France and embraces Catholicism in 1948; she and Chouraqui end their marriage but remain close for the rest of her life.

1948 Together with Jules Isaac and several others, Chouraqui is involved in the founding and organization of the first Amitiés judéo-chrétiennes (Jewish-Christian Friendship Associations).

On November 15, André successfully defends his doctoral thesis on the legal aspects of the creation of the State of Israel (almost certainly the first PhD to be devoted to this topic).

1949 During a trip to Italy, Chouraqui meets with high-ranking Catholic Church authorities for the first time.

1950 Publication of his first two books: *L'Introduction aux Devoirs des Cœurs de Bahya ibn Paqûda* and *La Condition juridique de l'Israélite marocain*.

July and August: visits Israel for the first time.

1951 Publication of Chouraqui's first translation of a biblical book (the Song of Songs).

1953 American Jewish Commitee publishes an English edition of *La condition juridique de l'Israélite marocain*.

1955 His French translation of the Psalms is published with his commentary.

1956 July: Private audience with Pope Pius XII and discussions with senior Vatican officials about possibilities for relations between the Catholic Church, the Jewish community, and the State of Israel.

Restoring the Gospel's Jewish Voice

          Chouraqui meets Israeli Prime Minister David Ben-Gurion.

          With the support of the Israeli government, Chouraqui helps to establish the Comité pour l'Entente religieuse en Israël et dans le monde (Committee for Religious Understanding in Israel and in the World), bringing together Jews, Christians, and Muslims to begin interreligious conversations.

1957   Works on a Galilean kibbutz with Annette Lévy, who will become his second wife.

          Death of his father Isaac.

1958   Chouraqui decides to relocate to Jerusalem.

          Second marriage, to Annette Lévy, and their move to Jerusalem.

1959   Ben-Gurion asks Chouraqui to join his cabinet, with responsibilities for the integration of new immigrants. Chouraqui becomes part of Ben-Gurion's "biblical circle," which meets in Ben-Gurion's home to share biblical scholarship with the Israeli leader.

1961   Adopts Israeli citizenship and becomes a dual French-Israeli citizen.

1963   As a representative of Ben-Gurion, Chouraqui visits the Vatican and delivers a memo regarding Vatican-Israeli relations.

1964   Resigns from government several months after Ben-Gurion's resignation.

1965   Is invited to the Vatican for the vote on Vatican II's declaration *Nostra aetate* (on non-Christian religions)

A Chronology of André Chouraqui

              Agrees to run for deputy mayor of Jerusalem alongside Teddy Kollek and wins; takes on responsibility for relations with the city's religious groups.

1967   The Six-Day War, whose frontier runs dangerously close to Chouraqui's home.

1969   *Letter to an Arab Friend* is published and wins the Prix Sévigné.

1971   June: Chouraqui serves as a go-between at a tense time between Israel and the Vatican regarding Church properties; Chouraqui tells the Vatican that its main Jerusalem property, the Notre-Dame Centre, will be returned to the Vatican. He engages in discussions with high-level Catholic officials.

              Publication of *Letter to a Christian Friend*.

1972   Retreats to the monastery of Latroun to begin his work of translating the Bible (both Old and New Testaments) into French.

1974   The first ten volumes of *La Bible Chouraqui* are published.

1977   Completes his work on *La Bible Chouraqui*.

              March: Engages in discussions with the king of Morocco, which help to pave the way for the historic peace negotiations between Israel and Egypt (Anwar Sadat would travel to Israel in November).

              October: Presents the twenty-six-volume set of *La Bible Chouraqui* to Pope Paul VI.

1978   Widespread (but ultimately incorrect) rumors suggest that Chouraqui will be named the next president of Israel.

1979   Publishes *Ce que je crois* (*A Man in Three Worlds*), his first autobiography.

	Meets with Pope John Paul II to discuss interfaith and inter-state relations.
1981	Colette dies, with Chouraqui at her bedside.
1982	The first volume of *L'Univers de la Bible*, Chouraqui's annotated and illustrated edition of his translation, is published by Brépols.
1984	Chouraqui begins his translation of the Qur'an.
1985	The tenth and final volume of *L'Univers de la Bible* rolls off the presses, and the first one-volume edition of *La Bible Chouraqui* is published.
	December: Meets Pope John Paul II again; discussions about how to facilitate diplomatic relations between Israel and the Holy See.
1987	Completes his translation of the Qur'an and submits it to a team of scholars for review and comment.
1990	Publication of *L'amour fort comme la mort* (Love as strong as death), his second autobiographical work.
	Chouraqui's translation of the Qu'ran (*L'Appel*) is published, making him the first person in history to have singlehandedly translated the holy books of the three Abrahamic religions.
1991	Meets with the Dalai Lama.
	Receives the Prix Henri Hertz from the University of Paris for *L'Amour fort comme la mort*.
1992	Receives Honorary doctorate from the Catholic University at Louvain.
	Receives the Leopold Lucas award from the Evangelical University of Tübingen for his biblical translation.

A Chronology of André Chouraqui

1994	Chouraqui is made a Commander of the French Legion of Honor by President François Mitterrand.
1996	October: While in Paris, Chouraqui suffers a serious stroke, but gradually recovers and is able to return to his work.
	December: The city of Jerusalem recognizes Chouraqui as a Citizen of Honor of Jerusalem (*Yakir Yerushalayim*).
2001	Publication of his third autobiography, *Mon Testament: Le feu de l'Alliance* (My testament: The fire of the covenant).
2003	Receives the Raoul Wallenberg Prize, a human-rights award, from Argentina's ambassador to Israel.
2007	André Chouraqui dies at the age of ninety and is buried in Jerusalem.
2020	The city of Jerusalem announces that it is naming one of the city's squares as "Place André Chouraqui," to honor its former deputy mayor and distinguished citizen. The dedication itself occurs in June 2021, in the presence of André's family and the French ambassador to Israel.

FOREWORD

Yehezkel Landau, DMin

Murray Watson has offered us all an extraordinary gift: a book-length portrait of a remarkable man and his unique contribution to interreligious engagement in our time. And since its subject, Nathan André Chouraqui, is little known to English readers, this book will open many Anglophone eyes, minds, and hearts. Watson is himself a multilingual scholar and interfaith educator, so he is well suited to be Chouraqui's biographer and textual commentator. For that intellectual and spiritual service, we are in Watson's debt.

    I got to meet André Chouraqui and learn about his work when I joined the staff of the Israel Interfaith association in 1980. In that capacity, I helped organize educational programs that brought together people from different faith communities in Israel/Palestine. Chouraqui attended meetings of the Association, as well as other interfaith gatherings in Jerusalem sponsored by the Ecumenical Theological Research Fraternity in Israel or the Rainbow Group. On one memorable occasion, I was invited to his resplendent home on Ein Rogel Street—overlooking the Temple Mount/Haram ash-Sharif, the Mount of Olives, Mount Zion, and the Hinnom Valley—for a conversation related to a forthcoming activity of the association. In that meeting, and whenever I interacted with him, I found Chouraqui to be a charming, humble, erudite interlocutor with an infectious *joie de vivre*.

    I had moved to Jerusalem from the United States two years earlier, linking my own life story to the homecoming of Jews from the four corners of the earth. As an interfaith practitioner and educator, I sensed even before arriving in Israel that the reestablishment of Jewish sovereignty in the Holy Land had created radically new conditions and opportunities, both for Jewish self-understanding and for relations between Jews and other faith communities, especially Christians and Muslims. With a critical mass of Jews residing once again in the land, and the power dynamics altered by Jewish statehood, Jews could engage their Abrahamic siblings with greater self-confidence, gradually overcoming the haunting memories of past vulnerability and suffering. Within this historical context, I saw André Chouraqui as an exemplar of Jewish self-assurance in relations with Christians and Muslims.

As Watson demonstrates, Chouraqui's own homecoming journey is worthy of a full-length biopic. He was born in Algeria in 1917, and he died in Jerusalem in 2007. In the intervening nine decades, he lived a uniquely multicultural, international, and generative life. He held a variety of professional positions in such diverse fields as politics, international affairs, scriptural scholarship, and interfaith relations. A man of many gifts and wide influence, Chouraqui's primary literary legacy lies in his scriptural translations—of the Hebrew Bible, the New Testament, and the Qur'an—whose shared aim was to transform engagement with sacred texts into an act of interfaith solidarity. (Watson notes that Chouraqui was "the first person in history to have singlehandedly translated the holy books of the three Abrahamic religions"). Throughout his colorful life, which spanned almost a century of horrific wars as well as liberation movements overturning colonialist regimes, Chouraqui maintained a hopeful attitude, rooted in his unwavering faith in humanity's capacity to overcome conditioned trauma and enmity and to create a more peaceful world.

Chouraqui's prolific literary output included three autobiographical works. His first was published in 1979 under the French title *Ce Que Je Crois* (What I believe) and translated into English as *A Man in Three Worlds*, published in 1984.[1] In the prologue to that volume, Chouraqui reflected on the three continents where he spent significant portions of his life:

Foreword

Africa, where I was born at the hour when it was preparing to win its independence, in the place where this independence was most dearly bought;

Europe, where I made my studies in law and in oriental languages in Paris, from which I soon had to flee to take part in the battles of the Resistance;

Asia, finally, where I have returned to take part in the rebirth of a country [Israel], my own, erased from the map twenty centuries ago by Roman imperialism. Counselor of Ben-Gurion during the last years of his government, Deputy Mayor of Jerusalem [working with the legendary Teddy Kollek] at the hour of its unification in June, 1967, in my maturity I have changed not only my continent, but my language and my culture, stripping myself of the old man I had been in my lands of exile, to be reborn on the glistening rocks of my Judea. (5, emphasis added)

Chouraqui then commented on the linguistic aspect of these geographical transitions:

This experience of returning to my spiritual wellsprings, my linguistic origins, my own land and my true culture I have chosen, at the age of forty, in full consciousness of what I was doing. I have deliberately changed my continent and my language; daily, from now on, speaking the Hebrew that I have had to relearn, and no longer the French and Arabic that were my native tongues. I have stopped writing from left to right, and must now draw my letters from right to left. A detail, you will think, but it is one that radically affects the inner equilibrium of a man. Gradually, this Jerusalem in which I have been living for twenty years has made of me another man. I had come here to put my life in accord with my thought and my beliefs. I shall say, then, what the new man I have become believes, speaking from my wellsprings in Jerusalem.

Restoring the Gospel's Jewish Voice

> What I am talking about is a change, a conversion, a return, which has renewed all my being and my thought, finally making possible, carried by the great currents of contemporary history, the sum total of a name and a destiny. (5–6)

The name whose sum total he was alluding to, Nathan André Chouraqui, reflects the Hebrew, Greek, and Arabic roots of his multicultural identity. Those origins yielded three distinct, but overlapping, worldviews that made up Chouraqui's cultural inheritance and that are reflected in the sacred texts that he devoted decades to translating and interpreting. Chourqaui's own explanation of his name was "God has given a man from the East." For him, the significance of this three-part name unfolded toward greater accuracy and authenticity as his life progressed. In a profound sense, he grew into that name more fully as he matured and added more cultural layers to his personality.

Chouraqui's understanding of identity, as a dimension of human existence forged from the crucible where history and destiny meet, resonates strongly with me. For I have also lived on three continents: South America, North America, and Western Asia. I, too, "returned" (or, in Jewish terminology, "ascended") to Jerusalem as an adult to become an Israeli citizen and deepen my Jewish commitment. In the same introduction to his 1979 autobiography, Chouraqui linked his own existential journey to the first Biblical patriarch in this ironic passage:

> Blame Abraham for my natal Algeria, torn between Christians, Moslems, and Jews, all of whom claim to be his children; for western racism, that mortal illness [it is not clear to me where the patriarch's impact and culpability lie here—YL]; for my departure from France and my return to Jerusalem. Yes, blame Abraham for my deep-rooted Jewishness, my faithfulness to my people of Israel, my studies in Paris at the Rabbinic School of France—and my departures, like him a big-tent nomad, constantly

Foreword

on the roads of more than twenty-four of the countries of our tiny and splendid planet. Blame Abraham for what I believe and what I do, what I say and what I write. (2)

As someone who also views *Avraham Avinu/Abuna Ibrahim* as a primary role model, even with the serious shortcomings depicted in Genesis, I share Chouraqui's self-understanding as someone following in the patriarch's footsteps. And we share another faith commitment rooted in the Abrahamic tradition and amplified by the later Hebrew prophets: working to heal the tragically conflicted relationships, reinforced by mutual ignorance, among the patriarch's spiritual heirs—Jews, Christians, Muslims, Druse, Bahá'ís, and others.

Also, like Chouraqui and Murray Watson, I have sought to understand Jesus of Nazareth within his own context as a first-century Jewish teacher, preacher, healer, and visionary leader. Chouraqui was among the cadre of Scripture scholars and exegetes over the past generation who have helped both Christians and Jews reevaluate the place of Jesus within the ambivalent relationship between the two faith communities. Reading the Gospel texts anew, as Jewish homiletical literature, has brought about a mutual reappraisal of Jesus and his teachings. Acknowledging Jesus as a faithful Jew and a rabbinic sage reclaims the Galilean for Judaism and the Jewish people;[2] and, at the same time, such a stance repositions Jesus for Christians as a distinct voice within the spectrum of Second Temple Jewish orientations. Overall, Chouraqui's scholarship helps Jews and Christians, along with Muslims, appreciate Jesus as a unique figure who can help bridge the tragic divides separating the Abrahamic faith communities.

Chouraqui's death in 2007 deprived the world of his ebullient spirit and his expansive knowledge of the Abrahamic traditions. But his literary legacy—poetry, fiction, philosophical essays, political commentary, and above all his French translations of the Tanakh, the New Testament, and the Qur'an—will live on forever. Now many more readers, including interfaith educators and activists, will be inspired by his intellectual brilliance and his towering spirit through this comprehensive study by Murray Watson. It is a study that is both deeply personal, examining Chouraqui's relationships with those around him, and sympathetically critical in exploring the writer's literary corpus, particularly his ten-volume masterpiece, *L'Univers de la Bible*. His translations could be both poetically inspiring and syntactically bewildering. Here are some illustrative lines from Watson's analysis:

> Chouraqui's passion for etymology, and his desire to mine the linguistic riches of words and concepts, has enlightened many but has also certainly confused others. His approach has had the benefit of bringing to the surface the "unvarnished" origins of biblical terms, often highlighting facets of their meaning that were traditionally either hidden or downplayed as unnecessary. His research has established new inquiries into apparently "settled" interpretations, and he has enabled readers without extensive training in biblical languages to appreciate the nuances and playfulness in those ancient texts.... While Chouraqui's extensive knowledge of languages permits him to draw on interesting linguistic trivia and make provocative juxtapositions, on a few occasions, Chouraqui's enthusiasm seems to have outrun his prudent judgement, and other scholars have pointed to questionable interpretations, or outright errors, among his linguistic conclusions. Biblical terminology has not always had the same meaning over many centuries, and the exact relationship of Jesus' (Hebrew? Aramaic?) words to our Gospels in Greek continues to spark debate. But it is a debate that Chouraqui would be happy to see taking place.

In rabbinic tradition, debates "for the sake of heaven" are valued as opportunities to deepen our understanding of God's will, transforming knowledge into wisdom. At our present historical moment, when religious differences are amplified in the service of toxic ideological and political agendas, we need visionary thinkers like Nathan André Chouraqui to help us overcome our tribalisms and triumphalisms, and

Foreword

to view one another as allies in the common religious task of consecrating life. Watson, in his preface, cites a statement by Chouraqui that succinctly expresses the motivation behind his scriptural translation project: "Only the original poetry of these Texts has the ability to strip away the political and ideological overlays from those books. I have sought to get back to the Message for what it is—and not for what certain people want to convince us it is. I knew that, as Jews, Christians and Muslims, what gave us life flowed from a common spring, and that we had to manage to drink from it together, in brotherhood."

Chouraqui's passion for interpreting sacred texts, as a way of elucidating humanity's most profound ideas and ideals, colored all of his writings. Murray Watson, too, is an impassioned biblical scholar and a cogent writer, conveying the essence of a topic with clarity and conviction. The book you are holding is a fitting testimony to the life and the legacy of an extraordinary man of deep conviction, inordinate compassion, and unparalleled devotion to peacebuilding through interfaith understanding. Read it and apply its lessons to your own life so that you, too, can be an agent of spiritual healing in a conflicted world that yearns for exemplars of humble, yet powerfully transformative, faithfulness.

ACKNOWLEDGMENTS

This book represents the completion of a journey that began in a library in Jerusalem, and that has lasted more than twenty years. During those years, André Chouraqui has been a constant companion in my studies, a teacher and a mentor in my interfaith efforts. Although we never had a chance to meet in person, Chouraqui's vision has guided and inspired me—and continues to. I am deeply grateful to his wife, Annette, for her kindness in helping me to understand her late husband, for her hospitality and her support. I hope that this volume helps to expose a new, English-speaking readership to André's groundbreaking and visionary work, and to continue what he began.

I owe a huge debt of gratitude to my parents and family for their patience, encouragement, and love, especially for the many years that I spent overseas pursuing my graduate studies in Rome, Jerusalem, and Dublin.

Thank you to the late Bishop John Michael Sherlock, and to Bishop Ronald Fabbro, CSB, for making these studies possible, and for their friendship.

Thank you to the Rev. Dr. Peter Pettit, a good friend and cherished colleague, for his generous advice, encouragement, and dialogue, which helped me to restructure, hone, and improve this manuscript for publication.

Thank you to my dear friend Shawn Syms, for carefully reviewing and commenting on the many iterations of this manuscript, for guiding me to find a less academic and more inviting voice, and for his unfailing enthusiasm and support.

To all of my colleagues and friends who have indulged me as I shared my passion for Chouraqui's work: Thank you for your patience and good humor. I hope you will find this book interesting and worthwhile!

M. W.

> Αἰνέσωμεν δὴ ἄνδρας ἐνδόξους καὶ τοὺς πατέρας ἡμῶν τῇ γενέσει...
> ἡγούμενοι λαοῦ ἐν διαβουλίοις καὶ συνέσει γραμματείας λαοῦ,
> σοφοὶ λόγοι ἐν παιδείᾳ αὐτῶν....
> τὰ σώματα αὐτῶν ἐν εἰρήνῃ ἐτάφη, καὶ τὸ ὄνομα αὐτῶν ζῇ εἰς γενεάς
> Let us now sing the praises of famous men, our ancestors in their generations...
> those who led the people by their counsels and by their knowledge of the people's lore;
> they were wise in their words of instruction....
> Their bodies are buried in peace, but their name lives on generation after generation.
>
> (Sirach 44:1, 4, 14)

PREFACE

Nathan André Chouraqui. Have you ever heard of him? Chances are good that you haven't...*but you should*. Because he was far from an average man—let alone an average biblical scholar and translator.

André Chouraqui's identity was rich, complex, and multilayered. He was a Jew—whose mother tongue was Arabic. He was born in Africa—and later served as deputy mayor of Jerusalem. As a Sephardic Jew, born and raised in a multilingual household in Algeria, who is primarily known in the French-speaking world, the young Chouraqui was representative of a minority within a minority within a minority.

As a student under the colonial French education system, he was for a time an avowed atheist—who later undertook rabbinic studies in Paris. Despite his religious rediscovery, Chouraqui was a friend and onetime comrade in arms of the absurdist writer Albert Camus, who famously described religious faith as "philosophical suicide." Chouraqui's own spiritual reawakening coincided with his experiences during the Second World War; he was an active participant in the French Resistance against the Nazi occupation of France and the collaborationist Vichy régime, and was part of an underground network that smuggled children to safety, and provided aid to those fleeing Nazi persecution. In his own words, "If Hitler wanted to take my life because I was Jewish, at least I wanted to die with my eyes open, knowing what it meant to be Jewish."

His spiritual rediscovery was also spurred by his interactions with Christians and Muslims, and a burgeoning passion for interfaith harmony. Scholar, politician, activist, interfaith advocate…do you think someone with that sort of uncommon pedigree might have an interesting take on the Holy Book? In fact, André Chouraqui is responsible for one of the most remarkable and provocative biblical translations of modern times: *The Chouraqui Bible*. Published between 1974 and 1977. As a twenty-six-volume set.

Because his work was in the French language, many religious scholars, interested laypeople, and interfaith advocates outside of the French-speaking world are not aware of the *La Bible Chouraqui* or its author. I'd like to help change that with this book.

I must admit that I initially discovered Chouraqui's work by a providential accident. In 2001, I was a graduate student in Jerusalem at the Dominican Fathers' École biblique et archéologique française (French Biblical and Archaeological School, the birthplace of the famous Jerusalem Bible). At the time, its world-class library was being renovated and modernized, and its collection was boxed up in storage; we students had to fan out across Jerusalem, to find libraries whose collections we could use for our course work and research. I was living with the Jesuits at the Pontifical Biblical Institute in a different part of the city, and it was in their library that I stumbled across Chouraqui's *L'Univers de la Bible*—his magnum opus—which included his translation, extensive interpretive notes and commentary, and a wealth of related photographs of artifacts from the world's greatest museums. As a student of the French language, at a French-language school, I was initially curious, and then—as I delved more deeply into Chouraqui's work and learned more about him—in turn, intrigued, impressed, and inspired. I used his work throughout that year, and never forgot the uniqueness and freshness of his translation and the brilliance of his overall scholarship, which profoundly deepened my own understanding and appreciation of the Bible. I did not

Preface

realize at the time that Chouraqui and his wife Annette were living just a few miles away from me.

When I had the opportunity to pursue doctoral studies several years later at Trinity College in Dublin, I was excited to be able to delve into Chouraqui's work—and his amazing personal vision—in greater depth over a period of several years. Unfortunately, he died before I had a chance to interview him; that remains one of my great regrets. I am grateful, however, to his wife Annette for her hospitality, and for the opportunity to discuss her husband's life and work at their home on Ein Rogel Street in Jerusalem. The more I have learned about André Chouraqui, the more I have been amazed and inspired by him, and I have had numerous opportunities to speak about him to various audiences, who are similarly impressed and inspired. This book is my attempt to introduce him and his work to an English-language audience.

In the first section, "Translation for transformation," I will introduce you to Chouraqui's viewpoint, motivations, and a few modern antecedents that influenced his efforts. Then we will dive right into a close reading of the theological and syntactical "nuts and bolts" of *The Chouraqui Bible* (Did you know that there are *two* Jerusalems? Or that Jesus wasn't really named "Jesus"?). Through detailed examples, we will see how Chouraqui adheres to some standards and traditions in the history of biblical translation and interpretation—and yet breaks with others. The Chouraqui Bible is, of course, a part of an overarching cultural history of biblical interpretation—still, I would argue that it is in a category by itself, unlike any biblical translation that either preceded or followed it.

And that's because of *who Chouraqui was*—his place in history, geography, language, and culture. So, in the second section, *Une vie très pleine* (A very full life), we will examine the contours of Chouraqui's uncommon biography, beginning with his humble beginnings in a small Algerian town, and eventually leading him to Paris, Jerusalem, and Rome. Finally, I'll share some thoughts on Chouraqui's legacy for today's flourishing global interfaith movement.

Restoring the Gospel's Jewish Voice

Today, around the world, dialogue between religions is commonplace and taken for granted. Since the Second World War—and especially since the 1960s—interreligious dialogue has become an important component of civil society in many countries. Religious leaders stand together and speak together, calling for peace, promoting justice and defending human rights. But we don't have to look back very far to realize this phenomenon is unprecedented—and therefore important to appreciate.

Religions have interacted for millennia. But friendly, positive, and mutually respectful relationships? That concept is really less than seventy-five years old. The interreligious harmony movement blossomed amid the social changes of the 1960s; but its foundations were laid earlier—in response to the atrocities of the *Shoah*, or Holocaust.[1] Many self-identified Christians had actively collaborated with the Nazi death machine. Beyond that, many millions of Christians had effectively ignored the genocide happening around them. So it's unsurprising that the public revelation of the full extent of the Shoah in the years immediately following the Second World War provoked a profound crisis of Christian conscience.

Surviving Jews were incredulous at the broad involvement of Christians in Nazi persecution; Christians were left to consider their guilt and grapple with their shame. How could such behavior be reconciled with the clear teachings of Jesus Christ—about active compassion for the vulnerable and weak (Matt 25:31–46) and about love of neighbor as the obligatory corollary of love of God (Matt 19:19; 22:34–40)? Christians were challenged to honestly acknowledge and confront what had happened. As the Indian novelist and political thinker Arundhati Roy has remarked, "Keeping quiet, saying nothing, becomes as political an act as speaking out. There is no innocence. Either way, you're accountable."[2] Or, as the Talmud states, "The one who can protest and does not, is an accomplice in the act" (*b. Shabbat* 54b).

It was in this context of moral ambiguity, suspicion, and self-examination that the International Council of Christians and Jews (ICCJ) was born. Between July 30 and August 5, 1947, a group of

Preface

sixty-three Jews, Protestants, and Catholics from a dozen nations gathered in the Swiss town of Seelisberg to take part in the International Emergency Conference on Anti-Semitism, the first major gathering of Jews and Christians since the war's end. During their deliberations, the participants considered a dossier of materials that had been prepared by the distinguished French Jewish historian Jules Isaac, examining the measures necessary to rectify distorted Christian views of Jews and Judaism (expect to hear more about Isaac within this book's pages). Their final statement, which has become known as the "Ten Points of Seelisberg," proposed a fundamental reorientation of Christian thinking on key theological and historical issues, with a view to improving interfaith understanding. Today, the ICCJ looks to Seelisberg as its founding moment, and most historians of religion point to it as a seminal event in beginning to change Christian attitudes toward Jews—and, by extension, toward other religions, too.

Jules Isaac was also one of the founders of the Amitiés judéo-chrétiennes, the network of Jewish-Christian Friendship Associations. And so was André Chouraqui. Drawing upon his own life experience in Algeria and France, Chouraqui made a conscious decision to dedicate his life to promoting understanding and respect among the Abrahamic faiths.

In France—and later in Israel—Chouraqui became a passionate and articulate advocate for interfaith engagement. His political career led him into the inner circle of Israel's founding prime minister, David Ben-Gurion, and, eventually, to two terms as deputy mayor of Jerusalem, which spanned the bloody 1967 and 1973 wars. Having borne witness to both these wars, as well as the Shoah, Chouraqui was no stranger to the *worst* of humanity, and yet he never ceased to promote and call forth the *best* of humanity. To him, genuine inter-religious dialogue was the solution to the ugliness, hatred, and violence he had repeatedly seen up close in his life. It was a vision he pursued relentlessly until his death in Jerusalem, in the summer of 2007.

Restoring the Gospel's Jewish Voice

With his religious upbringing and exposure to Arabic, Hebrew, and French as a child, it's no wonder Chouraqui was drawn to biblical translation. Even as a boy, he had been frustrated by what he perceived as inadequacies in the French Bibles he read, which he felt failed to capture the nuances, and the linguistic playfulness, of many Hebrew biblical texts. And Chouraqui decided that he would only fully understand Christianity "from the inside" if he had grappled firsthand with the meaning of its holy books, setting an instructive example for each of us who care deeply about interreligious understanding.

In a move that was undoubtedly ambitious—but also daring and apt to provoke scandal—Chouraqui embarked on a French translation of both the Hebrew Scriptures and the Christian Scriptures—*both* Testaments. His goal was to help his readers appreciate the connectedness of the two bodies of sacred literature—and to underscore the fundamental Jewishness of the New Testament for Christians…and for Jews.

He wanted to "restore the Hebrew voice" to the Bible—and a specifically "Jewish voice" to the New Testament—in some key ways: (1) "bending" the French language so that the pages of his Bible would more accurately reflect the linguistic textures of the ancient Hebrew, even if the results might sound awkward in the context of modern idiom; and (2) focusing on the ancient source texts and trying to accurately capture the meaning of words and stories they contain, so that readers would experience a Bible more accurately rooted in the times and places in which its events were both set and written about.

In this second regard, Chouraqui was consciously bucking a dominant school of biblical translation called "dynamic equivalence," which tends to adopt changes to structure and content such that the text will both flow more smoothly and be more comfortable and comprehensible to readers in their own language.

Chouraqui didn't want to spoon-feed parables; he wanted his readers to stop and think. He wanted to remind Christians that Jesus was a first-century Middle Eastern Jew—and not a modern European.

Preface

And as such, he hoped Jewish readers could also see the relevance of the New Testament for their own history. Chouraqui sought to highlight the linguistic and theological currents that linked the holy books of Judaism and Christianity, and to demolish assumptions and prejudices that artificially, and unnecessarily, held the two religions apart.

> Doubtless, it is from the multiple inheritances linked to my birth, and from the experiences of my youth, that I drew the strength of my desire: to bring back to life—in unity, around one and the same wellspring—what human beings had torn apart. The walls of hatred,...within which they believed they could find safety and refuge, must fall. My hope—of seeing those far off draw near,[3] to be united in the same love—was rooted in the search for my own identity. My translation of, and my commentaries on, the Hebrew Bible, the New Testament and the Qur'an are the work of my whole life, which I have entrusted to my moment in time. They mark the endpoint of years of delving into my own identity, and into the identity of people that I saw battling with each in endless theological disputes. This task—of delving into the roots that sustain us—forced me to reject certain myths, or to shed light upon them, through the necessary but never-ending work of re-reading the original texts....
>
> It is love for this ineffable Being [God] that I discovered in each Psalm, each verse of the Gospels, each *sura* of the Qur'an....Today, I have no legacy to offer, other than the love that I have discovered in Him. His love commands us to come forth, out of our ghettos, and to smash the myths which stand in the way of our freedom....Only the original poetry of these Texts has the ability to strip away the political and ideological overlays from those books. I have sought to get back to the Message for what it is—and not for what certain people want to convince us it is. I knew that, as Jews, Christians and Muslims, what gave us life flowed from a common

spring, and that we had to manage to drink from it together, in brotherhood.[4]

Not everyone is a fan of Chouraqui's Bible translation. It's far from elegant. But its passion is infectious. On every page, it challenges the reader to rethink received ideas about the Bible—and about the relationship of Judaism and Christianity. I have found it—and Chouraqui himself—richly inspirational, as both a scholar and as a Christian. Within these pages, I will do my best to show you why, and to convince you of the same.

P.S.—Oh, did I mention that he translated the Qur'an as well?

SECTION 1

TRANSLATION FOR TRANSFORMATION

מה נשתנה התרגום הזה מכל התרגומים ?
Why is this translation different from all other translations?[1]

1
THE WORD MADE STRANGE[2]

Now the whole earth had one language and the same words. In the story of the Tower of Babel, the Book of Genesis suggests (in Gen 11:1) that, in the far-distant, mythic past, our planet's inhabitants spoke a single language, understood by all—and that it was human arrogance and sinfulness that splintered that original unity, thus accounting for today's linguistic diversity.[3]

That legendary account is more likely making a theological and moral point than a historical, linguistic, or anthropological one. But in this twenty-first century of ours, there is indeed a multiplicity of mother tongues on our planet. While exact numbers for living languages are hard to nail down, reputable sources suggest that they number between 6,500 and 7,500. At least some portions of the Bible have been translated into roughly half of those languages, while full translations of the Bible exist in only 10 percent of them.

The English language enjoys a particular abundance of biblical versions, with more than four hundred distinct versions prepared and published since the groundbreaking work of John Wycliffe and his disciples back in the fourteenth century; several dozen have been made just since 1900. Most Western languages possess a healthy choice of translations (often at least a Protestant version and a Catholic version).

YET ANOTHER BIBLE TRANSLATION...WHY?

Since the 1400s, at least one hundred translations of the Bible have been made into the French language. Given that abundance of options, did the world really need another Bible translation in French? Well, André Chouraqui certainly thought so. And in setting himself to that task, he made an outsized contribution to both biblical scholarship and modern Jewish-Christian relations. With his *Chouraqui Bible*, he joined a long line of Jewish translators of the Holy Book—but he extended his efforts in an unconventional direction, when he chose to *also* translate the New Testament. In his translational work, he consciously embraced a model that favored the structure and linguistic roots of the original over easy vernacular readability. And in both regards, it's his distinctive intent that drove his creation of one of the most groundbreaking, provocative, and original Bible translations of the past century.

The French *Bible Chouraqui* has had its share of both friends and foes. It's been praised as robust, refreshing, innovative, and even startling...and dismissed as quirky, eccentric, unpolished, and even undignified. Its creator was celebrated with honorary doctorates, prestigious awards, and words of praise from popes, presidents, and prime ministers—and he was dismissed as being out of his league, naive, and a dilettante, dabbling in a field best left to professional exegetes. Since his death in 2007, Chouraqui's distinctive model of biblical translation had continued to draw rave reviews, and to provoke criticism and disdain. It isn't a version of the Bible that leaves people indifferent. The French call someone who deliberately stirs up debate an agent provocateur; in the world of Bible translation, that is precisely what André Chouraqui was.

During the Passover Seder meal, one of the key questions asked is, Why is this night different from all other nights? (in Hebrew: *Mah nishtanah ha-layla ha-zeh mikol ha-leilot?*). Similarly, we might ask, What is it that makes *this* translation different from all *other* translations? What did André Chouraqui do differently—and why?

Certainly, his Bible was different because its translator's *goals* were different from those of many previous translators. It was a translation intended to raise important linguistic and theological questions, and then to bring people—especially Jews and Christians—together in order to discuss them. It stands out from the entirety of mainstream French Bibles that preceded it because Chouraqui saw biblical translation as a way to foster dialogue and conversation, to break down barriers, misunderstandings, and prejudices. Even if it could not re-create the primordial unity of pre-Babel humanity that Genesis portrays, nevertheless he felt that it could make an important contribution to healing wounds and disarming age-old conflicts. The Bible *could* be a source of greater unity and respect, rather than a weapon in a theological flame war.

The *Chouraqui Bible* was inspired by a vision of interreligious dialogue that matured in its creator's mind over decades. Thus, it cannot be adequately understood apart from the biography of its translator, who lived at the crossroads of some of the most interesting moments of modern history. Later in this book, we will delve more deeply into Chouraqui's life to enrich our understanding of his work. In this chapter, however, we set his translation work in historical and methodological context, and in the next chapter, we will turn the pages of his Bible for a close reading and examination of its distinctive linguistic strategies.

So...מה נשתנה (*Mah nishtanah...?*) What makes it different? First, its methods and intent set it apart from the efforts of other Jewish Bible translators, both historical and contemporary.

Before the Common Era, the Jewish Scriptures (which were still evolving into their final fixed form) had already been translated from Hebrew and Aramaic into a collection of Greek versions that today we call the Septuagint.[4] And within two centuries of Jesus's life, alternative Greek versions were circulating; we know of the ancient versions named for Aquila, Symmachus, and Theodotion, which the brilliant Church father Origen (ca. 185–ca. 254) reproduced and studied as part of his massive biblical research tool, the *Hexapla*.[5]

Although Hebrew, as the predominant language of Jewish Scripture, has always enjoyed a privileged place in Jewish biblical study, over the centuries Jewish scholars also produced various vernacular translations, such as the 1917 JPS (and 1985 New JPS) versions in English, and the Zadoc Cahn and *Bible du Rabbinat* translations in modern French. In ancient times, Jewish renderings of biblical texts into Aramaic (a related Semitic language) produced a body of literature called *targums*. While the targums often incorporate interpretive traditions, many of them also adhere very closely to the original text and tend to produce versions that we would today often refer to as "literal," or in keeping with what is called the "formal equivalence" model. Paul V. M. Flesher and Bruce D. Chilton, two specialists in ancient Jewish literature, explain in *The Targums: A Critical Introduction*:

> The Targums...emphasize formal correspondence without necessarily implying semantic correspondence.... [That is:] the translation aims primarily to reproduce the form of the original, and only secondarily its original meaning....It is more important that the grammatical form and structure of the original be reproduced....Aramaic Targums tend to represent nearly every linguistic element of the Hebrew text in the same order as they appear there....The Jews of late antiquity saw Scripture's form as important, as well as its meaning. After all, if God inspired the Hebrew Bible, then the way those words were put together, as well as their relationship to each other, was as important as the words' meaning. They knew that grammar, as well as semantics, could determine correct interpretation and understanding. So they worked to preserve it.[6]

Historic translations from the Hebrew Bible into other languages made by Jews—especially the translation into Greek by Aquila (completed around 130 CE)—traditionally leaned in a more literal direction. *Word order* and *linguistic structures* were considered divinely inspired and meaningful, so it was important to reproduce these characteristics of the source text, even when this might yield a less-than-elegant final product. As one scholar says, "Aquila's translation was quite woodenly literal, so that his grammatical constructions were at times foreign to Greek,"[7] and a standard edition of the Greek Septuagint remarked that "Aquila's translation of the Bible must on occasion have proved altogether incomprehensible to non-Jews."[8]

Language is the bearer of meaning, and so it's necessary to capture as much of the mother tongue as is feasible. But—as any translator will tell you—this is a demanding (and ultimately elusive) goal. Centuries later, Chouraqui followed in that much older Jewish tradition. Keeping with his passionate interfaith convictions, Chouraqui focused on the New Testament, but with a motivation and approach to its books that differed starkly from many of the Jewish translators who had preceded him.

A NEW TESTAMENT ANEW

Over the course of nearly twelve hundred years, portions of the New Testament—and sometimes entire Gospels—had been translated into Hebrew. Of this there is ample evidence.[9]

But let's look at who engaged in these efforts—and why. Generally, such translations were made by one of three categories of Jews:

1. Jews who had converted to Christianity, and wanted to make arguments about the truth of Christian claims in a language that would be accessible and persuasive to their former coreligionists

2. Rabbis and scholars who, conversely, to defend their communities against heavy Christian pressure to convert, translated New Testament texts in order to study them and respond knowledgeably and adequately in debates

3. Some Jewish converts to Christianity who (it has been posited) may have translated New Testament passages

into Hebrew (and Hebraized Latin) to hold on to their Hebrew culture and not lose it entirely[10]

So prior engagement with the New Testament by Jewish translators had primarily been for purposes of either proselytization or self-defense, or perhaps out of a sense of nostalgia. Not so with Chouraqui. As a proud Jewish believer and a leading citizen of the modern State of Israel, he was coming to the New Testament freely, willingly, and out of a sense of intellectual curiosity and interreligious conviction. His goal was neither to promote conversion nor to defend a beleaguered Jewish community, and so he approached the New Testament with confidence and a certain intellectual distance.

Jewish engagement with the New Testament might be unusual or controversial, but none of those previous Jewish translators had been working in an independent Jewish state, in the context of a Christian theological rethinking that had been occasioned by the horrors of the Shoah. Chouraqui was, therefore, a unique individual living at a unique period in world history.

Translating the Bible is itself an ambitious undertaking. Doing so with an eye to fostering Jewish-Christian dialogue and friendship seemed to many a Herculean (and perhaps hopelessly idealistic) task, given the often painful history of the two faiths. But perhaps Chouraqui remembered the famous words of Rabbi Tarfon in the Mishnah: "You are not obliged to finish the work—but neither are you free to turn aside from it" (tractate *Pirqe Avot* 2:16). He could not singlehandedly transform that tortured relationship…but he felt obliged to make the contribution he—and he uniquely—could.

A BIBLE "IN THE LANGUAGE IN WHICH IT WAS WRITTEN"

As we shall explore in greater detail later in this book, when he began this work in the early 1970s, Chouraqui had just recently stepped down from a very active life as a leading Israeli political figure, first as a cabinet minister in the government of David Ben-Gurion, followed by two terms as deputy mayor of Jerusalem (which

The Word made strange

overlapped with the wars that Israel fought in 1967 and 1973). After more than fifteen years at the center of the rough-and-tumble world of Israeli politics, he was tired and disillusioned. The time had come for silence and reflection, and to return to a project of which he had long dreamed—grappling with the words and meaning of every verse of the Bible.

> The compulsion to translate seized me when I was a child in our synagogue of Aïn-Témouchent, where I tried to penetrate the meaning of the Hebrew Bible and of our prayers, following them in bilingual editions. As an adolescent, to translate meant for me to penetrate the meanings of the ancestral heritage that my parents were struggling to bequeath to me. Then came the time of making comparisons between what I understood the texts to mean and what the translations said of them. For my guidance, I re-established the meaning of words and the harmonies of the rhythms as they resounded in my head, in a radically Frenchified Hebrew. Thus were born my translations of [the eleventh-century Jewish philosopher-rabbi] Bahya ibn Paqûda's *Duties of the Heart*, of the Song of Songs and of the Psalms [published in the 1950s]. My vocation as a translator would probably have stopped there if I had not come to settle in Jerusalem. My project of translating the Bible could be achieved, now that I had under my feet the earth of the Prophets and of the Apostles, and that I could converse with the Bible in the language in which it was written. Now that Hebrew had become once more my mother tongue, I could see more clearly the defects of my previous translations; they were smothered under a cloak of customs, embroidered through thousands of years, so that the forms and meanings of the original text could hardly be recognized....A revolution was needed, if, by that term, one understands a return to

the origins. Yes, to liberate man, we must begin by liberating the word.[11]

Chouraqui had dreamed for decades about translating the entire Bible, and that is what he did, with a singular drive and focus. Chouraqui indicates that he began his translation work in earnest in 1972, and the first part of his translation was already being published in January 1974, with ten volumes issued in that year alone. In the realm of biblical translation, this sort of individual output is truly extraordinary.

For long periods during 1974 and 1975, he retreated to the silence of the Cistercian monastery of Latroun (northwest of Jerusalem), where he dedicated himself to completing his translation of the Old Testament and, eventually, the New Testament as well. Chouraqui handwrote the first draft of his text, which he then had typed up and forwarded to colleagues who could critique and correct his work. He would subsequently review and revise his materials on the basis of their feedback, and send them corrected copy to consider, a patient back-and-forth process that continued until he and they were satisfied, and he felt he could submit the typescripts to his publishers, Éditions Desclée de Brouwer in Paris.

It was a punishing schedule but, by early 1977, Desclée had published the entire twenty-six-volume first edition of *La Bible Chouraqui*. Certainly, there are few biblical translators, ancient or modern, who could claim to have translated such an enormous corpus of material in such a short span of time (especially without access to today's computer technology!). Over the years, Chouraqui incorporated suggested corrections in his text, improved and polished it, almost until his death; later editions would expand and comment on his earlier work. The core of the translation, however, remained largely stable, rooted in his specific vision and methodology, which was earning him a large and growing readership in France and across the French-speaking world.

The Word made strange

TO ADAPT, OR TO REFLECT?

Chouraqui's longing to "converse with the Bible in the language in which it was written" drove countless choices that he made, as we will explore in significant detail in the next chapter. And it aligned with a theoretical camp in the world of translation practices.

For much of the post-Renaissance period, the ideal for many vernacular translators has been to produce a text that flows smoothly and expresses itself beautifully in the receiving language. Many European translations deliberately aim at expressing the biblical message in a form considered suitably refined by the standards of their own great literature. Some versions, such as the modern Jerusalem Bible, are the fruit of translators, literary scholars, and poets working together, deliberately seeking out an idiom that captures the flavor, and draws upon the genius, of the tongue in which the translation will be heard. American translation theorist Lawrence Venuti has noted in his book *The Translator's Invisibility* that the ideal for many modern European translators and publishers has been to create an "illusion of transparency," the impression that one is reading, not a translation, but the original text itself:

> A fluent translation is written in English that is current ("modern") instead of archaic, that is widely used instead of specialized ("jargonization"), and that is standard, instead of colloquial ("slangy"). Foreign words ("pidgin") are avoided….Fluency also depends on syntax that is not so "faithful" to the foreign text as to be "not quite idiomatic."…A fluent translation is immediately recognizable and intelligible, "familiarised," domesticated, not "disconcerting[ly] foreign."[12]

In addition to the aesthetic aspirations of this approach, it falls into the dynamic-equivalence translation model—it privileges the structure and meaning of the *destination language* over that of the *source language.* The result is often a version that, while stately, is quite "comfortable" for the reader, making ancient Babylon or first-century Galilee seem surprisingly close to home, and thus making the biblical message feel more accessible to its contemporary readers.

In the twentieth century, however—and especially in its final decades—translators of both Testaments, Jews, Christians, and others, were beginning to step away from this polished, dynamic-equivalence tradition, and to explore once again what the contours of a more rugged, more literal type of translation might look like, one that strove to capture more of the distinctive flavor of the original biblical languages. This devotion to the ancient texts, structure, and meanings has come to be known as the *formal-equivalence model*. This is often a deliberately political choice; as Venuti argues, this type of "foreignizing" translation "can be a form of resistance against ethnocentrism and racism, cultural narcissism and imperialism." Especially in our world today, it can represent an ethical statement as well: "Insofar as foreignizing translation seeks to restrain the ethnocentric violence of translation, it is highly desirable today, a strategic cultural intervention in the current state of world affairs, pitched against the hegemonic English-language nations and the unequal cultural exchanges in which they engage their global others." The translator's choice of method can (and often does) express a vision of modern geopolitics.

Such translations would, of course, be much less "comfortable" and user-friendly; they would require their readers and listeners to struggle at times with words and concepts that were unfamiliar. They would need to "find their way" in a strange new land where anachronisms would be minimized, in which the cultural and linguistic "otherness" of the text was accentuated. Aesthetics might need to yield to a new historical and social sensitivity—or perhaps a *new* aesthetic was waiting to be born.

וּבִמְלֹאת הַיָּמִים שָׁלַח הָאֱלֹהִים אֶת־בְּנוֹ יְלוּד אִשָּׁה וְנָתוּן תַּחַת יַד־
הַתּוֹרָה

*When the fullness of time had come, God sent his Son,
born of a woman, born under the guidance of the Torah*

(Galatians 4:4; Hebrew from the Delitzsch New Testament)

2

JEWISHNESS FOR JESUS

His passion for fidelity in translation was one of the things that led Chouraqui to embark on his own new biblical translation. André grew up in a devout family that moved comfortably among Arabic, Hebrew, Aramaic, and Ladino and, even as a boy, he noticed that the richness of the Hebrew text had become lost or tempered in translation, hemmed in by centuries of received, "official" interpretations. In his mind, it was necessary to "dust off" the Bible, to allow it to speak in a fresh and relevant new way that could be compelling for contemporary readers.

But his second—and perhaps more important—impetus lay in his desire to bring Jews and Christians together around study and discussion of the Bible. He knew that, for many Jews, the New Testament was, at best, irrelevant and, at worst, hostile territory because of its perceived anti-Jewish tone and the ways biblical interpretation had been used against the Jews throughout history. And he knew that, for many Christians, the Old Testament had been largely reduced to a mine of proof-texts and messianic foreshadowings of Jesus—that its primary purpose was understood to be the buttressing of Christian theological claims. A great gulf had come to separate Christians and Jews in terms of approaches to the Bible, leaving little common ground for fruitful conversation. Their theological presuppositions about each other largely precluded serious shared engagement over the meaning of their holy books, even those they shared. Their histories fostered reticence and suspicion of one another.

Chouraqui, however, knew that things could be different. Witnessing the Second World War firsthand, as a student and Underground member, had fostered in him a personal passion for breaking down historic barriers of hostility and misunderstanding between the two faiths. His own profound study of the Bible—both Old and New Testaments—had highlighted many of the shared theological and linguistic threads that united the two sections of Scripture. He believed that translating key terms consistently could help his readers to appreciate the inner unity of these holy books—to appreciate connections where, perhaps, only differences had been obvious before.

INRI: JESUS OF NAZARETH, KING OF THE JEWS[13]

And he wanted his readers to appreciate something that many people take for granted today, but that was still quite radical in the early 1970s: *that the New Testament is fundamentally Jewish literature.* He wanted his Jewish friends to begin to appreciate the quintessential Jewishness of Jesus and the New Testament—and he wanted his Christian friends to do the same, so that the New Testament might become a bridge between the two faiths, instead of the wall it had heretofore been. While that was not yet an entirely mainstream concept (especially in Israel), neither was it completely without precedent.

Earlier in the twentieth century, Jewish authors had begun to explore the question of Jesus's place within Second Temple Judaism. In the mid-1920s, Claude Montefiore famously argued, in *The Synoptic Gospels*, that one day Jews could reappropriate the New Testament as a monument of Second Temple Jewish literature—without, of course, embracing its theological content: "[The New Testament] is a book which, in very large part, was written by persons who were born Jews. Its central hero was a Jew. Its teaching is based throughout—sometimes indeed by way of opposition—upon the teaching of the Old Testament."[14] A similar comment was made by liberal rabbi Lewis Browne in the 1940s, in his justification for including the teachings of Jesus in his Jewish anthology, *The Wisdom of Israel*:

> The New Testament has a place in this anthology because it obviously contains much wisdom, and this wisdom is unmistakably Hebraic. Those who uttered it were all born in Israel, and so were virtually all those who recorded it. The fact that they were generally regarded as dissidents, and that their teachings were eventually branded heresies, does not in the least reflect on the essential Jewishness of the spirit animating their lives and words.[15]

By the late 1960s, prominent Jewish scholars were increasingly writing about the historical and cultural background of Jesus, including Schalom Ben-Chorin's 1967 *Brother Jesus: The Nazarene through Jewish Eyes*, and the work of scholars David Flusser and Geza Vermes. Could a new paradigm of biblical translation provide a common ground upon which to discuss the things that *united* them as Jews and Christians (and, inevitably, those that *separated* them)? Chouraqui felt the time was ripe for a new approach to the age-old tensions between the two faiths. And he had definite ideas about what that approach should look like.

CHOURAQUI'S MODERN-DAY ANTECEDENTS

Many scholars today point to the groundbreaking 1936 German translation of the Hebrew Bible by Martin Buber and Franz Rosenzweig as a first dramatic shift away from the more traditional "literary" model of Bible translating, opening a new and different path. Working together in the late 1920s, Buber and Rosenzweig sensed a need for a translation to contrast with Martin Luther's sixteenth-century German version, which had acquired both a theological and linguistic canonicity in German culture, shaping the

German language in a way analogous to the influence of the 1611 King James Version on English.

Their focus would not be on *vernacular readability*; on the contrary, their approach *highlighted* the "otherness" of the text, attempting to reproduce, as far as possible, the structure and flavor of the Hebrew, for readers unacquainted with the Jewish Scriptures in their original language. This edition of the Tanakh would, where necessary, "bend" German syntax and vocabulary to adhere more closely to Hebrew idioms; it would not be easy for biblically literate Germans to initially encounter. It would require a certain surrender, a willingness to be stretched in unaccustomed ways, to step out of one's own time and place, and to rediscover the Hebrew Scriptures in a fresh—and hopefully engaging—new form, in which the Bible's *original* voice could shine through more clearly, in syllables that had been molded to fit a more ancient mentality. As Princeton University's Leora Batnizky has noted, "By doing away with 'smoothed-over conceptual language,' by creating a process of defamiliarization, the Buber-Rosenzweig translation sought to produce shocked attention in its readers."[16]

The first volume of Buber and Rosenzweig's shared effort appeared in 1925, and their collaboration ended in 1929 with the latter's death. It was not until 1936 that the Buber-Rosenzweig translation of the Torah was first published, in a Germany that was already becoming permeated with Nazi ideology. Perhaps not unexpectedly, most critics savaged the new translation, which embraced a more consciously *Jewish* form of the text and seemed to call into question the authoritative nature of Luther's Bible, an icon of Lutheran religion and of German national pride, inextricably interwoven with the German language itself.

Buber and Rosenzweig's approach was roundly condemned, and the resulting translation was considered a strange German-Hebrew hybrid that many found awkward or distasteful. Some insisted that its language was excessively "archaized" or "Orientalized," and that these qualities made of it a version destined only for a small élite of intellectuals, rather than for the common people whose common language had been the inspiration and guiding criterion of Luther's efforts. Others saw it as minimalistic or overly analytical, its abruptness having lost any sense of the poetry or music of German, and so rigidly focused on form that it lost much of its emotional impact.

The rise of the Nazis, and the prospect of imminent war, interrupted Buber's work, and in 1938 he emigrated to Mandatory Palestine. But the project had kindled an inextinguishable fire in his mind and heart, and he would return to it several times over the subsequent decades, publishing the final volumes of his translation in 1961, only four years before his own death in Jerusalem. By then, the world was a very different place, and the radically changed political, social, and literary landscape—coupled with Buber's substantial reputation as a religious philosopher—yielded a more nuanced and receptive appreciation of his work.

Considering Buber's examination of the essentially *dialogical* nature of human beings, his translation took on an even deeper significance. This relationship of differentiation and respect, which Buber famously expressed in terms of the "I-Thou" dyad, is also at the heart of the religious person's interaction with the transcendent Other. Might it not *also* have ramifications in terms of engagement with an ancient sacred text like the Bible, which can only be properly understood and valued once its specific "otherness" has first been acknowledged—that is, when it's understood (in some sense) as a "Thou" to be encountered? In a manner anticipating some strands of modern intertextual hermeneutics, Buber's translational philosophy could suggest that the text is itself a type of "interlocutor" to be engaged. But this first presupposes a certain "distancing" from the text: a respectful awareness of the cultural and historical gulf that separates us from the biblical period.

In his discussion of Buber, the University of Toronto philosopher Robert Gibbs writes, "The commitment to displaying the difference of the earlier text to its new context reflects the way that *dialogue is not about shared experiences, but about the risky bridges that do not reduce difference*" (emphasis added).[17] Buber and Rosenzweig's

Translation for Transformation

work demonstrates how certain styles of translation can themselves serve as icons and paradigms of interreligious and intercultural dialogue, can "incarnate" the principles that Buber and his disciples had tried to lay down.

Even since the publication of the Chouraqui Bible, several new biblical translations have appeared that also draw inspiration from Buber and Rosenzweig's style of translation. Perhaps the single best known of these is Everett Fox's volume *The Five Books of Moses: A New Translation*, first published in full in 1990. Fox's translation—the premier volume in the Schocken Bible series—places great emphasis on literary and linguistic fidelity to its Hebrew source, highlighting wordplays in the text, and translating with a directness and ruggedness that has enabled many English readers to discover the "Hebrew voice" in the Torah in a way previously impossible. Fox is forthright about the debt he owes to Buber and Rosenzweig, and the relation between their earlier translation and his own:

> [This work] was conceived as an act of homage to the Buber-Rosenzweig translation; at the beginning, I desired solely (and rashly) to bring their accomplishment over into English....*The Five Books of Moses* is still very much in the Buber-Rosenzweig tradition....It is...the child of Buber-Rosenzweig....It may also be seen as an attempt to bring the work of Buber-Rosenzweig into a new era of Bible scholarship, and as an artistic endeavor in its own right.[18]

Fox's rendering of a portion of God's command to Noah in Genesis 6 (vv. 17–22) offers a glimmer of the ways in which his translation differs from many others:

> As for me, here, I am about to bring on the Deluge, water upon the earth, to bring ruin upon all flesh that has rush of life in it, from under the heavens, all that is on earth will perish. But I will establish my covenant with you: you are to come into the Ark, you and your sons and the wife and

your sons' wives with you, and from all living-things, from all flesh, you are to bring two from all into the Ark, to remain alive with you. They are to be a male and a female (each), from fowl after their kind, from herd-animals after their kind, from all crawling things of the soil after their kind, two from all are to come with you, to remain alive. As for you, take for yourself from all edible-things that are eaten and gather it to you, it shall be for you and for them, for eating. Noah did it, according to all that God commanded him, so he did.[19]

In the twenty-five years since its original publication, Fox's translation has gained wide scholarly acclaim for its innovative, thought-provoking, and revelatory approach, and has provided a paradigm from which other translators have drawn inspiration.

THE JEWISHNESS OF JESUS

Almost midway in time between the Buber-Rosenzweig German translation of the 1920s and 1930s and the Everett Fox English translation of the mid-1990s, there was the child-of-the-1970s *Bible Chouraqui*. Each translator was deliberately trying to capture linguistic and theological aspects of the biblical text that they felt had previously been lost or obscured in earlier translations. Each wanted his readers to appreciate that the Bible is, in many ways, a strange and foreign land. This demands mental and cultural adjustments on the parts of actively engaged readers, to avoid reading their own assumptions into the text in ways that can be anachronistic and misleading.

Chouraqui's work coincides with the beginnings of the late-twentieth-century effort to reinsert Jesus into his cultural and religious milieu, to reconceptualize Jesus as a faithful first-century Jew, living and preaching in the Middle East. Unlike earlier Christian scholarship that downplayed, ignored, or explained away Jesus's Jewishness, today's so-called Third Quest for the Historical Jesus takes that Jewishness as one of its starting points.

Translation for Transformation

The 1978–2005 pontificate of Pope John Paul II was one of the great catalysts in modern Jewish-Christian relations. Throughout his papacy, John Paul tried to remind both Jews and Christians of Jesus's integral Jewishness in his official teachings (emphasis added):

On May 15, 1982, in an address to university professors in Coimbra, Portugal, he said,

> God, in revealing himself to the Chosen People, made use of a particular culture; Jesus Christ, the Son of God, did the same thing: *his human incarnation was also a cultural incarnation.*

On April 11, 1997, when speaking to the Pontifical Biblical Commission, he said,

> *Jesus's human identity is determined on the basis of his bond with the people of Israel*, with the dynasty of David and his descent from Abraham....*Thus he became an authentic son of Israel, deeply rooted in his own people's long history.*...To deprive Christ of his relationship with the Old Testament is therefore to detach him from his roots and to empty his mystery of all meaning.

On October 31, 1997, inaugurating a Vatican-sponsored colloquium on "The Roots of Anti-Judaism in Christian Settings," he said,

> *Those who consider the reality that Jesus was a Jew and that his milieu was the Jewish world as merely incidental cultural facts* (for which it would be possible to substitute another religious tradition, from which the person of the Lord could be detached without losing his identity) *not only misconstrue the meaning of salvation history but, more radically, call into question the very truth of the Incarnation.*

Jewishness for Jesus

Notre Dame University's John Meier, one of the most respected and encyclopedically knowledgeable scholars of the historical Jesus, saw Jesus's Jewishness as essential, from both a scholarly perspective and a theological one:

> I would suggest that one definite gain [from the search for the historical Jesus] that must be incorporated is...*the true and thorough Jewishness of Jesus*. From the Council of Chalcedon onwards, the touchstone of genuine Christian faith in Christ has been the formula "truly divine and truly human." Yet it is not too much of an exaggeration to say that, in defense of the "truly divine," the "truly human" has sometimes been obscured or swallowed up.... What the Third Quest can supply as an aid to regaining the Chalcedonian balance is the firm *basso continuo* of "truly Jewish" as the concrete, historical expression and underpinning of the theological "truly human." To speak in Johannine terms: when the Word became flesh, the Word did not simply take on an all-purpose, generic, one-size-fits-all human nature....*The Word became truly flesh insofar as the Word became truly Jewish. No true Jewishness, no true humanity*. Hence, contrary to the charge that the high Christology of orthodox Christianity necessarily leads to a covert theological anti-Semitism, I think that a proper understanding of the Chalcedonian formula, illuminated by the Third Quest, necessarily leads to a ringing affirmation of the Jewishness of the flesh the Word assumed. Even if the Third Quest has no other impact on contemporary Christology, the emphatic reaffirmation of the Jewishness of Jesus will make the whole enterprise worthwhile. Something lasting will have been gained.[20]

Like many Jewish translators before him, Chouraqui is fascinated with etymology—with the root meanings of the Greek words and phrases he is translating in the New Testament—but he is also intrigued by the originally *Semitic* voice that he hears behind them, which he wants to bring to the surface for modern readers. He wants to root Jesus's words and teachings in the world he inhabited, and he doesn't hesitate to hypothesize when he feels the Greek may have inadequately captured those Hebrew or Aramaic underpinnings.[21] His efforts allow for a Jesus who more naturally belongs in that first-century world, and whose words can inspire and challenge in strikingly new ways:

> Rediscovering the Hebrew or the Aramaic behind the Greek words, and the exact thought they are expressing; re-situating the idea that has been thus extracted into its semantic context, and the facts being described into a historical reality that has too often been forgotten: *this* is our way of reading (and thus of translating) the New Testament. It allows for a stripping-away of what encases the text, which our minds can then see in its striking originality—as a covenant that is new once more.[22]

The French verb that Chouraqui uses to express this process—*décaper*—suggests "sanding down" an object, stripping off accumulated layers of paint or varnish, to get to the original material underneath it. While this approach is admittedly fraught with difficulties and uncertainty (even for lifelong scholars of those languages), Chouraqui wanted his translation to forcefully remind Christians that their Lord and Savior, in his humanity, had been a son of the Holy Land, and that his culture and language were quintessential parts of his identity and mystery that Christians needed to take seriously in their theologizing. *Behind the Greek of the Gospels, there was a Jewish individual speaking a Semitic language.*

Understanding these two intersecting trends—a more linguistically purist, less "polished" mode of translation, and a radical attentiveness to the implications of Jesus's Jewishness—is key to appreciating Chouraqui's way of rendering the New Testament Gospels. Chouraqui's entire biblical translation is worthy of in-depth study, and several francophone linguists and exegetes have published articles, and whole books, discussing his unique approach to the Bible.

But for the purposes of Jewish-Christian dialogue, I believe that it's his translation of the four Gospels that can be the most enlightening and helpful, both in terms of appreciating his guiding principles and seeing how he concretely puts them into practice. It is an excellent starting point for understanding Chouraqui's method and seeing how his renderings compare with other, more familiar translations—and *why*.

There are many ways in which Chouraqui tried to capture the specifically Jewish context of Jesus and the Gospels, by pointing his readers to customs and cultural details, both large and small, that capture the *ambience* of Galilee, Judea, and Jerusalem. Although many contemporary Christians may lack the in-depth cultural familiarity and historical background to appreciate them, those details have the potential to be revelatory—to shine a light on Jesus's personality and teaching—because they root him in that particular time and place (and Christian theology argues that the time and place of Jesus's incarnation are not random or accidental, but theologically significant).

In the next chapter, we will look at several of those examples, to try and understand *why* Chouraqui does what he does, and how it can be helpful to resituating Jesus in his original cultural landscape. We will closely examine his strategies for uncovering some of the rich truths contained in ancient words and ancient meanings. Through his work, Chouraqui sought to help Abraham's children find their way back to each other, in respect, friendship, and dialogue. It was a type of translation that could only make sense in the late twentieth century—a contribution that André Chouraqui was uniquely qualified to make. Together, let's explore what makes it different, and why, and *how*.

> אבי, אל חי שמך, למה מלך משיח לא יבא?
> *My father, named Living God, why will the King Messiah not come?*
> דעו מאביכם כי לא בוש אבוש, שוב אשוב אליכם כי בא מועד.
> *Know from your Father that I will certainly not tarry; I will certainly return to you when the appointed time comes.*
>
> (A palindromic theological question posed to the great Jewish exegete Avraham ibn Ezra, to which he provided a palindromic reply.)[23]

3

ENTER THE HEBRAIC MATRIX

What makes Chouraqui's Bible distinctive and different? Its uniqueness stands out most clearly when compared with other translations (although these comparisons will necessarily be imperfect since we are comparing him with standard *English* translations). But even in translation, the style and texture of his version comes through. Let's look at some of the ways in which Chouraqui creatively highlights the Jewish or Hebraic matrix of Jesus, and of the Gospels more generally, and seeks to aid his readers in appreciating the richness—and complexity—of the biblical text.

A MIND-"ALTAR"-ING EXPERIENCE

By contrast with most other versions, Chouraqui sets out to amplify the strangeness, or alterity, of the text, to jar the reader into awareness that she is journeying through "foreign territory," necessitating a reorientation on the *reader's* part. He invites his modern readers to intellectual humility and respect—but also to curiosity and wonder. In doing so, Chouraqui participates in a tradition of exploration of the rich vocabulary of the ancient Bible. While translators employing a dynamic-equivalence framework lean in the direction of

Enter the Hebraic matrix

eloquence in the *target* language, formal equivalency experts draw our attention to the particular cadences and differences of the *original* languages, which were often characterized by wit and cleverness: punning, double-entendres, and nuanced word choices, which it is very challenging (and often impossible) to reproduce in another language.

Let's briefly consider a few examples. The Canadian literary theorist (and ordained United Church of Canada minister!) Northrop Frye notes, for instance, "[An] Aramaic pun is probably involved when John the Baptist says (Matthew 3:9) that God is able of these 'stones' (*ebhanim*) to raise up 'children' (*banim*) to Abraham."[24] John F. A. Sawyer, an expert in early Christianity, adds, "A less obvious example of this, requiring a knowledge of Hebrew as well as Greek, occurs in Acts 28:1: 'After we had escaped, we heard that the island was called Malta' (Greek *Melita*; cf. Hebrew *melitah*, [for] 'escape')." Some of the most extensive—and often controversial—studies of theorized biblical wordplay have been done by scholars such as Maurice Casey, Claude Tresmontant, Éric Edelman, and Joachim Jeremias, as part of their efforts to reconstruct the Semitic original versions of Jesus's words.[25]

WHAT'S HIS NAME AGAIN?

Surprisingly, there is no "Jesus" in Chouraqui's Bible. That's because there was no one in that world who was called by that name. And he's not the only one! People, places, and things throughout the *Chouraqui Bible* are given the names by which they were most likely known in their own times. For Christian readers, this can be startling and disruptive. Which is just what Chouraqui wants. Let's take a closer look.

While you will never find "Jesus" (or "Jésus") in Chouraqui's translation, you'll regularly encounter *Yeshua'* (in Chouraqui's French: *Iéshoua'*). Jesus's mother, Mary, is once again *Miryam*; her husband is *Yosef* (for Chouraqui: *Iosseph*). (Because certain letters are pronounced differently in English versus French, I will occasionally need to adjust the spelling of Chouraqui's transliterations, so they will be more easily understandable to English-speaking readers.)

The names by which many Westerners today call the Nazarene—the French *Jésus*, the Italian *Gesù*, the Spanish *Jesús* and so on—are all based on a Latin transliteration (*Iesus*) of a Greek rendering (*Iēsous*, Ἰησοῦς) of an originally Semitic name (*Yeshuaʿ*, יֵשׁוּעַ), itself probably a shortened form of Joshua [יְהוֹשֻׁעַ]. This means that the form "Jesus" is at least three steps removed from the name by which the historical *Yeshuaʿ* was familiar to his contemporaries.

This has cultural implications and consequences for our interpretation of several important passages. Although most modern readers are unaware, many proper names in the Bible are short *phrases* in Hebrew. Knowing the etymological roots of such names frequently allows us to grasp an aspect of what the biblical authors were conveying about the character or the mission of a biblical figure. Classic examples of this would be the link made between the personal name Adam and the Hebrew word *adamah* (soil or ground), or the connection between the name Isaac [*Yitzḥak* in Hebrew; "he will laugh"] and the verb "to laugh" [*tz-ḥ-k* in Hebrew, or צחק]; terms related to laughter and jesting occur several times in that patriarch's life story.

As the Slovenian exegete Jože Krašovec has noted in *The Transformation of Biblical Proper Names*:

> In the Hebrew Bible, there are nearly ninety more or less formulaic expressions in which information is given on the circumstances involved in the naming of persons, groups, peoples or places, and what the significance of their name was....These biblical passages are often called "folk (popular) etymology." The unique feature of folk etymology in the Hebrew Bible is the causal connection between a particular event and the naming of a person or locality....In most cases, etymological explanations of biblical proper names involve a play of words expressing the essence of the event and of the name derivations in the biblical texts.[26]

Enter the Hebraic matrix

Knowing this can help modern readers to appreciate the otherwise impenetrable Matthew 1:21 (emphasis added):

> She will bear a son, and *you are to name him Jesus*, for *he will save* his people from their sins.

This verse plays upon two related forms of the Hebrew three-letter verbal root יש״, *y-sh-ʽ* (referring to *saving* or *healing*). The original name of Jesus approximates a future tense verbal form, meaning something like "He will save" or "He will heal." What Matthew offers here is a subtle play on words—you are to name him *Jesus* ("he will save"), for *he will save* his people from their sins. Without an awareness of this pun, the angelic command to Joseph remains opaque, and the point is missed. Jesus's declaration in Luke 19:9 (in the story of Zacchaeus) that "today, salvation has come to this house" suggests similar wordplay. Jesus [*Yeshuaʽ*] is obviously the one who has come, and the Hebrew word for salvation is *yeshuʽah*, spelled very similarly and from the same verbal root, with only a slight difference in pronunciation.[27] In this vein we can also understand the challenge to the crucified Jesus to "save" himself (Matthew 27:40; Luke 23:35)—to *do* that which both his reputation and his very name seemed to point to, to *show* that "God will save." Obviously, these linguistic connections are lost in both Greek and English. But many scholars believe that Matthew's original community was predominantly Jewish,[28] and presumably *they* would have understood—and smiled at the linguistic connection.

Speaking of Jesus, Chouraqui renders the well-known Palm Sunday acclamation to him, *Hosanna* (in Matthew 21:9, 15; Mark 11:9, 10; and John 12:13) as a transliteration: the cry *Hoshaʽna*, literally, "Save [us], please!" derived from the same basic root [*y-sh-ʽ*], to which *-na* (a suffix suggesting a petition or prayer) is added—addressed, presumably, to one viewed as a Savior. For many Christians, the "pleading" aspect of *Hosanna* (visible in Psalm 118:25, for example) has largely been lost; it has come to be seen strictly as an acclamation of praise and victory.

Mary's name in Chouraqui's Bible allows for a rich resonance between the Old and New Testaments. As early as the 1920s, Christian scholars were already exploring the biblical figure of Miriam as an important point of reference for understanding the New Testament's Mary. As the German Jesuit scholar Franz Zorell noted, "Undoubtedly, the name of the Blessed Virgin Mary was given to her by her parents honoring the great person of Miriam, the sister of Moses and Aaron.... Probably a desire for rebirthing the People Israel...led Joachim and Anna[29] to bestow this name."[30]

Contemporary Christian scholars have rarely expressed interest in pursuing this line of thinking, however. In the words of the Barcelona-based biblical scholar Luis Díez Merino,

> In the New Testament, the parallelism of Moses and Jesus is often highlighted, but it's curious that in the New Testament Mary, the sister of Moses, doesn't appear as one of the prototypes that could offer a basis for other New Testament characters, especially for Mary, the Mother of Jesus, who bears her name....Jewish tradition has emphasized the role of Miriam, the sister of Moses, alongside the first savior of the people of Israel...but in the case of Miriam, the sister of Moses, and Mary, the mother of Jesus, it is strange that [typological parallels] have very seldom been invoked.[31]

Chouraqui's decision to retrieve Mary's Hebrew name reminds Christian readers of how deeply and inextricably the Christian story is rooted in the earlier story of the people of Israel; in so many cases, its storylines are woven with threads—characters and events—that are eminently familiar from the Old Testament.

Just as there are no Jesus, Mary, or Joseph (in those specific forms) in Chouraqui's New Testament, neither is there a John the Baptist (or, in French, *Jean-Baptiste*). Instead, we meet *Yoḥanan the Immerser*. Chouraqui thus draws attention to the original meaning of the ancient Greek verb *baptizō*—or in Hebrew, *taval* (טבל)—which denotes a "plunging" or "immersion" into a liquid. This connotation—

Enter the Hebraic matrix

clear to first-century Greek-speaking Christians—has been obscured in modern times because of the sacramental practices of some churches that rely on *sprinkling* or *pouring* (and not *immersion*) for baptism. The fact that an entire branch of Protestant Christians are called "Baptists" can make the sobriquet "John the Baptist" a bit confusing to some contemporary readers. The older baptismal tradition of immersion or plunging is inherent in the two epithets used for John in the Greek Gospels: *ho baptistēs* (the Baptist) and *ho baptizōn* (the Baptizer).

The original Semitic form of John's name—*Yoḥanan* (יוֹחָנָן) "God has been gracious/shown mercy"—evokes the etymologically-related Hebrew noun *ḥēn* (unmerited grace, favor) and the corresponding verb, *ḥānan* (to show mercy, unmerited grace, favor). Fittingly, for the author of Luke's Gospel and for the other evangelists, John is the one whose very conception is a demonstration of God's unearnable graciousness; he is to be the messenger of the grace and favor that God is preparing to reveal imminently to the world in the person of Jesus.

Other Semitic names are similarly transliterated by Chouraqui, in place of their more familiar English versions. For instance: the Apostle James, son of Zebedee, is now *Ya'akov ben Zavdi* (יַעֲקֹב בֶּן־זַבְדִּי); we English speakers are often unaware that James is actually a form of Jacob (James, in Latin, is *Jacobus*). Simon Peter is rechristened—or, one might say, "de-christened"—*Shim'ôn Petrôs* (שִׁמְעוֹן פֶּטְרוֹס). Chouraqui's choice here clarifies *Jesus's double entendre* in Matthew 16:18 (emphasis added):

> And I tell you, you are *Peter*, and on this *rock* I will build my church, and the gates of Hades will not prevail against it.

Chouraqui makes the wordplay explicit—conveniently, in French, the name Peter and the word for rock are the same: "You are *Petros* (Pierre)—and upon this rock (*pierre*)…I will build my community." The prophet Elijah is called by his Hebrew name, *Eliyahu* (אֵלִיָּהוּ), and David's son and successor as king is no longer Solomon but *Sh^elomo* (שְׁלֹמֹה)—illuminating that proper name's connection to the word *shalom* (שָׁלוֹם), meaning well-being and peace.

With these choices, Chouraqui highlights the history of skillful use of proper-name wordplay in the original Hebrew texts that was noted by (among others) the distinguished French biblical and Dead Sea Scrolls scholar Jean Carmignac:

> The Benedictus, the song of Zachary, is given in Luke 1:68-79. In Greek, as in English, the Benedictus, as poetry, seems unexceptional. There is no evidence of clever composition. But when it is translated into Hebrew, a little marvel appears.[32]

The Benedictus, reproduced by Luke (1:68–79), is composed of three stanzas. The second stanza has, as its first line, "to show mercy to our fathers"—where the expression "to show mercy" translates the verb *ḥānan*, which is the root of *Yôḥanan* (=John). And then the second line follows: "to remember his holy covenant"—where "to remember" translates the verb *zākar*, which is the root of *Zākaryah* (=Zechariah). And then the third line: "the oath which he swore to Abraham our father," which uses (in two different forms) the root *shāba'* (to swear, to take an oath), which is the root of *Elîshâba'at* (=Elizabeth). Is it by sheer coincidence that the second stanza of this poem begins with a triple allusion (subtle but seemingly intentional) to the names of its three protagonists: John, Zechariah, and Elizabeth? But this evoking (of the verbal links with these names) exists only in Hebrew; it is not preserved when translated into Greek, French, or English. (Carmignac notes that, while these word games *could* also be Aramaic, they are less likely in that language, especially since the Aramaic verb "to remember" is *dekar* rather than *zākar*).

Carmignac is neither the first, nor the only, contemporary scholar to argue that there is a Semitic (probably Hebrew) text behind parts of our current Greek Gospels, whose contours can occasionally be discerned by careful analysis. Given even these few examples (which could be multiplied), is it any wonder that a passionate reli-

Enter the hebraic matrix

gious intellectual like Chouraqui was driven to understand every word and layer of meaning contained in the Bible?

WHAT'S IN A (PLACE) NAME? LOTS!

Chouraqui frequently uses ancient place names—many of which also (conveniently!) happen to be *modern* place names. He looks to the forms in which these regions and cities have been known for centuries, and even today (in many cases) can be found on modern road signs and maps in the Holy Land:

- Egypt *Mitzrayims* (מִצְרַיִם)
- Galilee *Ha-Galil* (הַגָּלִיל)
- Samaria *Shomrōn* (שֹׁמְרוֹן)
- Beersheba *Beer-Sheva* (בְּאֵר שֶׁבַע)
- Magdala *Migdal* (מִגְדָּל)
- Nazareth *Natzeret* (נָצְרַת)
- Bethlehem *Beyt-Lekhem* (בֵּית לֶחֶם)

Let's take a closer look at these ancient place names. First, note the unusual final *s* of *Mitzrayims*, by means of which Chouraqui wishes to signal that, in Hebrew, the name for Egypt ends with an unexpected *dual* ending (*-ayim*). Hebrew has *singular* nouns, *plural* nouns, and *dual* nouns, for things that naturally occur in pairs, such as parts of the body (you can expect to learn a lot more about Hebrew grammar and syntax in chapter 5, by the way). Traditionally, it has been suggested that the use of the dual form here probably referred to the two "kingdoms" (Upper and Lower Egypt) into which the country was divided in antiquity.

The name Galilee is derived from the Hebrew root *g-l-l*, meaning "circular" or "encircled area"—and thus, by extension, "district." Even today, its name in Hebrew is *Ha-Galil*, "the Galilee," and Chouraqui will simply use the form *Galil*. Centuries before Jesus, this northern region, on the border with other (non-Jewish) cultures, had become known (somewhat disparagingly) as *Galil ha-goyim*, "Galilee of the Gentiles/nations" (see Isaiah 9:1 and 1 Maccabees

5:15). In the generations before Jesus was born, "Western Galilee particularly had attracted scores of Syrians, Arameans, Phoenicians, and Greeks from Asia Minor, in addition to the Babylonian and Persian settlers who had been moved there in preceding centuries."[33] For this reason, there was "deep suspicion harbored by conservative Jews in the south toward their Galilean brethren in the north."[34] Speaking about "the *Galil*" in Jesus's time would have evoked memories and associations that "Galilee" does not for most Christian readers today. "At the time of Jesus, a Galilean in Jerusalem, however strong his Jewish credentials, would have felt and been perceived as to some degree a foreigner, and an easy target of suspicion."[35] *Galil* was shorthand for a cluster of ideas, negative or positive, depending on who was using it.

The ancient city of Magdala (only recently rediscovered by archaeologists) lies on the northwestern shore of the Sea of Galilee. John J. Rousseau, of the University of California (Berkeley), explains its etymological and cultural roots:

> [Magdala] was included in the territory of King Agrippa II by Nero and was renamed *Taricheae* or "salted fish." Its Aramaic name is *Migdal Nunya* (or Nunayah), "Tower of Fish" (*b. Pesahim* 46). The Talmud indicates that Magdala had a small harbor and a boat-building industry. It was a place of "wealth and depravity."[36]

In some cases, place names familiar to New Testament readers may differ noticeably from their originally Hebrew forms. Chouraqui both seeks to connect the two Testaments (by using a uniform spelling), and to unpack the meaning behind these names, which can be both interesting and instructive.

Samaria and Samaritans are very familiar to readers of the New Testament, but Chouraqui wants to connect them to the Hebrew name for the region: *Shomrōn* (and its inhabitants, transliterated by Chouraqui as *Shomronîms*). First Kings 16:23–24 states that the name *Shomrōn* derived from Shemer, the family from whom Israel's sixth king, King Omri, bought the land for his capital city. But it's

Enter the hebraic matrix

more likely derived from the Hebrew verb *shāmar*, which means "to keep watch over, guard, care for";[37] in St. Augustine's *Sermon 131*, in speaking about the Good Samaritan, he says, "The Samaritan passing by (it means 'guardian,' by the way) lifted him up onto his beast."[38] Since the Hebrew and Greek names differ significantly, Chouraqui wants his readers to be able to link the two—and to better understand a group that plays a significant role in biblical history (both positively and negatively).

With a population of nearly eighty thousand, Nazareth is currently the largest city in the Northern District of Israel (but *not* to be confused with Nazareth, the most popular hard rock band from the most northern country in the United Kingdom, Scotland!). Both scholars and laypeople have heard of "Jesus *of Nazareth*," and Matthew 2:24 says "he shall be called *a Nazarene*." But wasn't Christ born in Bethlehem, as opposed to the ancient village of *Natzeret* (which we think of as the hometown of his mother, Mary)? The late Father Bargil Pixner, a Benedictine monk and Holy Land archaeologist, has attempted to throw some light on this mystery:

> Many conjectures have been made as to what prophetic word Matthew was referring (in 2:23, "He shall be called a Natzorean"). The great Church Father St. Jerome…who had an excellent knowledge of Hebrew, suggests a very plausible solution. He mentioned in his commentary to this text that many of the Jews who believed in Jesus had a recollection that this word referred to the prophecy of Isaiah 11:1. The word 'shoot' (in Hebrew *netzer*) refers to the scion from the rootstock of Jesse, whose son was King David.…The title *Natzorean/Nazarene* thus alludes not so much to Jesus' *town of origin*, but rather denotes his *royal descent*.…So the designation of Jesus, the Natzorean, means in the first place that he was of Davidic lineage, rather than that he came from Nazareth. Matthew's prophetic word "He shall be called a Natzorean"

(2:23) should be taken to refer to Jesus as the *netzer*-shoot out of the tribe of David.[39]

Bethlehem obviously plays a central role in the Bible, as "David's town" and the birthplace of Jesus. However, as Father Richard R. Losch, an Episcopalian writer on biblical geography, points out, long before it acquired its more familiar Hebrew name, "Bethlehem" was originally named for a Canaanite divinity linked to the growing of food:

> Grain grew plentifully in the fertile valleys and was an important factor in Bethlehem's economy. The Hebrews, being faithful Jews, would naturally not honor the pagan fertility god Lachama. They called the town *Beth-Lechem*, meaning "House of Bread" or "Granary." Today it is still known as Bethlehem to the religious, but its official name is *Bayt Lachm* (Arabic for "House of Food").[40]

With all of this in mind, the folk etymologies associated with place names are a key component of biblical storytelling. Chouraqui had a passion for etymology, but for him it had a specific purpose: to enable modern readers of the Bible to grasp more clearly the historical and linguistic meanings behind these place names. This return to first-century Semitic names is one piece in a larger project, which is to stress—both for Jews and for Christians—*the inherent Jewishness of Jesus*, his message, and the primitive Christian tradition.[41]

Chouraqui must have known that these types of "linguistic archaeology" would upset or scandalize a certain type of religious piety. But his purpose—as an agent provocateur—is to shock and surprise Christians into a rethinking of the origins of their faith, bringing home to many—perhaps for the first time—Jesus's deep rootedness in the land, culture, and language of ancient Israel. These are also names (and forms of names) that are eminently familiar to many Jews and could enable them to see (and hear) Christianity in a somewhat different light, to perceive in it elements common to their *own* religious heritage.

Enter the hebraic matrix

One important question, however, is whether this "restoration" of Semitic names can *itself* constitute a form of selective anachronism, imposing upon later authors, writing in Greek, forms of names that they themselves might have been unfamiliar with, or would never have used themselves. Inasmuch as the cultural background of each evangelist—not to mention possible Semitic sources or influences, and the impact of layers of editing—remain hotly debated among scholars, it's impossible to answer this question definitively. For his part, Chouraqui chooses *historical* accuracy (i.e., the form in which a name was likely used in its own original setting) over *literary* accuracy (i.e., the form that the evangelist or final editor would have had in mind). This is one of the criticisms that have been leveled against his work.

For readers unfamiliar with Hebrew, Chouraqui's rendering can be a helpful bridge to a better understanding of some of the less immediately obvious linguistic and theological connections that the evangelists are making regarding Jesus, his identity, and his mission. Opening our eyes to these ancient nuances of language and meaning can allow us to reimagine the Christian Gospels in new ways—and can nudge us to learn more!

כָּל־ סוֹפֵר מְלֻמָּד לְמַלְכוּת הַשָּׁמַיִם דּוֹמֶה לְאִישׁ בַּעַל־ בַּיִת הַמּוֹצִיא
מֵאוֹצָרוֹ חֲדָשׁוֹת וְגַם יְשָׁנוֹת
Every scribe who has been trained for the kingdom of heaven is like the master of a household who brings out of his treasure what is new and what is old (Matthew 13:52).[42]

4

RESURRECTING MORIBUND THEOLOGICAL VOCABULARY

One of Chouraqui's primary motivators was a belief that certain key biblical terms had become fossilized through familiarity and overuse. Over centuries of French translation, expressions in both Testaments became divorced from their original meanings or were overly Christianized. Many terms had become "canonized" through long-time Christian use, employed theologically in ways that Chouraqui knew summoned up incorrect or misleading images that were no longer rooted in the concreteness of Jesus's original Semitic expressions. He aimed to help rectify that.

So it comes as quite a shock for the Christian reader to discover that the most common theological and biblical terms in the Gospels have been effectively sidelined by Chouraqui. His disruptive decisions are clarified considerably by the explanatory notes in his ten-volume *L'Univers de la Bible*, his most complete edition of his translation. As the reader progresses, his revisions both provoke new insights and offer a sense of liberation and freshness. That linguistic and theological reinvigoration was Chouraqui's stated purpose. Let's explore.

WHERE'S THE PRIEST?

The concept of priesthood doesn't play as central a role in the Gospels as in the Hebrew Scriptures, but it's there—frequently because of mentions of "the chief priests" among those who were opposed to Jesus. Luke specifies that John the Baptist's father, Zechariah, is a priest of the division of Abijah (Luke 1:5–8), and it is to "the priests" that Jesus sends cleansed lepers for formal acknowledgment of their healing (Luke 5:15; 17:14). Forms of the Greek *archiereus*, or high priest, occur eighty-three times in the Gospels—and the simple form *hiereus* (priest) occurs eleven times.

Yet, today when we think "priest," we often think of Catholic clergy. Not many people bring to their reading of the Gospels the understanding that priesthood has a much longer history and was originally an ancient *Jewish* institution. Chouraqui, having lived much of his life among Catholics in colonial Algeria, and in France, knows this. In his translation he is consciously focused on conveying an idea of the Temple priesthood as it would have been understood by a Second Temple Jew. For him, the terms most frequently used to translate "priest" in Greek and Latin (*presbyteros*; *presbyter*; *pontifex*) won't suffice.

The first, *presbyteros*, is the linguistic root of both the French *prêtre* and English *priest*. But in the Gospels, the term is used only with reference to the leading elders of the Jewish community. The association of *presbyteros* with a formal class of Christian leader is a development in the decades after Christ, as witnessed by the so-called Catholic Epistles of 1–2 Timothy and Titus. Chouraqui translates *hoi presbyteroi* as "the Elders," looking back to the origins of *presbyteros*; it's the comparative form of the Greek adjective *presbys*, "old; advanced in years."

The second term, *pontifex*, is associated with the pagan priests who served the Roman pantheon of gods. It's associated with their role as mediators between common people and the gods (*pontifex* means "bridge builder"). Interestingly, the title for the chief Roman pagan priest, *pontifex maximus*, or supreme bridge builder, was adopted by the Roman Church after 1453 as one of the official titles of the pope. The abbreviation *Pont. Max.* was used after the pope's name on carved inscriptions and Vatican coinage until the recent papacy of Benedict XVI.

Given its pagan origins, Chouraqui rejects *pontifex* as incompatible with the ancient Jewish understanding of the priesthood. In its place, he translates occurrences of the Greek *hiereus* with a word drawn from older French documents but uncommon in French usage today: *desservant*.

In eighteenth- and nineteenth-century references, *desservant* was a term used for the cleric who was the incumbent of a usually rural parish, who "served" or "ministered to" (from the French verb *desservir*) the surrounding area. The traditional Hebrew term for a temple priest, *kohēn*, seems to be derived from a verb that means "to officiate in a religious capacity; to serve as a priest"; it's a term specifically linked to liturgical service, and the French *desservant* is similarly limited in its scope: "*desservant* is used only in speaking about leading services or seeing to the functions of a chapel or an assigned parish."[43] The unfamiliarity of *desservant* (as a noun) avoids the anachronistic associations of the more common *prêtre*, or priest.

But the accuracy and relevance of Chouraqui's decision is debatable. Is a term for the pastoral work of small-town Catholic priests in the 1700s (who often remained in place for decades) an accurate analogy for the work that Jerusalem's priests (serving in rotation) did in the monumental splendor of the Second Temple—to which hundreds of thousands made an annual pilgrimage to pray and offer sacrifice? His use of a European Catholic term from an entirely unrelated period (to try and shed the "Catholic veneer" of another historical term) has provoked some and perplexed others. It could be an example of a worthwhile principle—taken too far.

RABBIS MULTIPLYING

The term *rabbi* occurs, in Greek transliteration, only fifteen times in the Gospels (Matthew 23:7–8; 26:25, 49; Mark 9:5; 11:21; 14:45; and John 1:38, 49; 3:2, 26; 4:31; 6:25; 9:2; 11:8). Insufficient, says Chouraqui. He expands on the meaning of the word in challenging ways in his translation, using it far more broadly, and far more times, than a Christian is used to seeing in the pages of her Bible.

Resurrecting moribund theological vocabulary

There are typically fifteen rabbi references in Matthew, Mark, and John. And the related form *rabbouni* occurs twice, in Mark 10:51 and John 20:16. This second term has often been used interchangeably with the first, notes Herman N. Ridderbos in *The Gospel According to John*: "'Rabbouni' literally means 'my teacher' or 'my master,' but it's used elsewhere simply as an equivalent to the common word 'Rabbi.'"[44]

By contrast, Chouraqui employs *rabbi* fifty-three times in his Gospels—the expected fifteen times, but also including the evangelists' use of the Greek noun *didaskalos* (teacher), most often as a form of respectful address. Using this title with reference to Jesus obviously resonates linguistically with modern Jewish readers, for whom *rabbi* is a familiar term and role ("leading teacher") in their congregations; it establishes an immediate connection and inserts Jesus into a well-known Jewish category. Numerous recent scholarly works, both Jewish and Christian, have portrayed and discussed Jesus under this rubric.[45]

But is "rabbi" an accurate rendering of *didaskalos* throughout all four of the Gospels? And was this Hebrew term employed during the lifetime of the historical Jesus—if so, in what sense?

The question of the meaning and historicity of the term *rabbi* is an old and vexed one. The traditional Jewish view, attested most famously in the 987 CE letter of Sherira Gaon of Pumbeditha (ca. 900–1000) to Jacob ben-Nissim, is that *rabbi* was a distinctly Palestinian Jewish title (as opposed to *rab* among the Babylonian Jews), but one that did not come into use *until* the gathering of scholars in the town of Yavneh, in the years after 70 CE.[46] It was during this period, when the surviving Pharisaic leadership was slowly morphing into a more rabbinic type of Judaism, that a formal "laying-on of hands" (*smikha*, or "ordination") was instituted by Yochanan ben-Zakkai (ca. 1–80 CE), by which someone was formally recognized as a learned scholar who could be referred to by the term *rabbi*.

On this basis (and based on the lack of *rabbi* as a title in the earliest strata of postbiblical Jewish literature), the traditional view has been that using *rabbi* in the Gospels is anachronistic, reading back into the first third of the first century practices and vocabulary that developed only decades *after* the time of Jesus.[47] In a series of *Jewish Quarterly Review* articles in the 1960s, scholars Solomon Zeitlin and Hershel Shanks debated this question fiercely, Zeitlin maintaining the traditional view and Shanks arguing against it.

Shanks acknowledged that, because of the limited pool of Hebrew and Aramaic literature from the period, it's impossible to be definitive. But he argued that the use of *rabbi* as a title in the last third of the first century was not an invention out of thin air, but a development of a term already in use—though likely as more of a title of respect and courtesy for a distinguished person, rather than a formal title implying study and an authorized teaching mandate.

This less formal usage—*rabbi* approximating our modern "Sir," or "Your Honor"—is essentially what we see in the Gospels. Further, Shanks argues, the presence of the term in transliteration in later Gospels—when the shift was already well underway from a predominantly *Jewish* community to a *Gentile* one—is hard to explain on the initiative of the evangelists, who were then forced to explain the meaning of this foreign term to their readers (as John does in 1:38, and in 20:16 for *rabbouni*).

The apparent interchangeability of *rabbi* and *didaskalos* in pre-destruction Judaism is confirmed, for Shanks, by Eleazar Sukenik's 1929 discovery of an ossuary (a stone box to hold the bones of a deceased person) on the Mount of Olives bearing on one side the name Theodotion in Hebrew lettering, with the Greek title *didaskalou* (belonging to the teacher) on the other side, presumably the Greek equivalent of the Hebrew *rabbi*.

Shanks's position of forty years ago has been borne out by Shaye J. D. Cohen, a distinguished scholar of Jewish history, on the faculty of the Harvard Divinity School. In a 1981 archeological and inscriptional study, Cohen examines all occurrences of *rabbi* and its cognates (*rab*, *ribbi*, etc.) found in extant inscriptions or monuments up to the seventh century (including three pre-70 ossuaries from Jerusalem). His conclusion:

Resurrecting moribund theological vocabulary

> The term "rabbi" is ambiguous. It may be either a popular designation for anyone of high position, notably—but not exclusively—a teacher, or it may be a technical term for someone who has been "ordained" and has achieved status and power within that society which produced the Mishnah, the Talmudim, and related works....Practically all Semites used the word *rab* and its forms to designate individuals of rank, and we have no reason to assume that every Jew so designated helped to write the literature and shape the Judaism we call rabbinic....For centuries, "rabbi" remained a popular title which could describe individuals who were not part of that Hebrew and Aramaic-speaking society which produced the Talmud.... If we allow the term "rabbi" to include more than just the Rabbis of the Talmud, we admit that even in Israel, where Rabbinic influence was strong, many Jews were led by men who might not have found favor in the eyes of those who were establishing what was to become, but still was not, "normative" Judaism.[48]

In that context, we don't need to posit the existence of a formal class of duly authorized Jewish teachers called "rabbis" to accept that the term was used for Jesus as a title of deference and respect, both by his followers and those who seek his counsel. Commenting on the controversy, the American biblical scholar Bruce Chilton notes in "Mapping a Place for Jesus" (emphasis added),

> The reluctance to use the category of "rabbi" in order to assess Jesus is to some extent understandable. That term can and has been used anachronistically, to impute the organized Rabbinate of the Talmud to the first century. In principle, however, that anachronism should be dealt with just as we cope with such terms as "messiah" (or "christ") and "son of God." It is a commonplace of scholarship to alert readers to the fact that "messiah" during the first century did not bear the apologetic associations that developed quickly in early

Christianity, and that "son of God" did not convey the ontological claims of the Council of Nicea....

John the Baptist is explicitly called "rabbi" in John 3:26, and Jesus is addressed that way more than by any other designation (Matthew 26:25, 49; Mark 9:5; 10:51; 11:21; 14:45; John 1:38, 49; 3:2; 4:31; 6:25; 9:2; 11:8). Still, scholars routinely object that Jesus "was not a 'rabbi' but a 'prophet' (eschatological or otherwise)" [E. P. Sanders, *Jesus and Judaism* (London: SCM; Philadelphia: Fortress, 1985)]. The Gospels suggest that, as he became known for his signs (Matthew 16:14; Mark 6:15; Luke 7:16; 9:8, 19; John 4:19; 6:14; 7:40; 9:17) and approached Jerusalem for the last time in his life (Matthew 21:11, 46; Luke 24:19), Jesus was indeed called a prophet, but not as persistently or routinely as he was called rabbi. In any case, the one address by no means excludes the other. That the term "rabbi" was current in Jesus' time is suggested by Daniel 2:48; 4:6; 5:11 and m. 'Abot 1:6, 16, as well as from inscriptions...[but] *being called "rabbi" did not involve an institutional qualification until a much later period*, well after the destruction of the Temple. When [John Dominic] Crossan and others compare Jesus to the popular philosophers of the Mediterranean world, especially the Cynics, their comparison may be helpful in general terms, although it seems clear that a Jewish teacher whose wisdom was valued would be called "rabbi."[49]

Following Shanks, I believe the evidence supports Chouraqui's translation of *didaskale* (the form used in direct address) as *rabbi* in direct address; it conveys a title of honor and a sense of deference to the guidance of a devout Jewish man considered a worthy spiritual teacher, biblical interpreter, or guide; this applies to its use both for Jesus and for John the Baptist. And in several passages where it's used indirectly, but as a title of respect by others—references to "your rabbi" or "the rabbi" in Matthew 9:11; 17:24; Mark 5:35; Luke 8:49; and John 11:28—Chouraqui's rendering is also justified.

Resurrecting moribund theological vocabulary

I cannot help but believe that Chouraqui goes too far, however, when he depicts Jesus as using the term to describe himself, and in using it more or less indiscriminately for *all* occurrences of the term "teacher" in the Gospels. While I can appreciate Chouraqui's desire for consistency in translation, it sometimes feels forced. This is another example where a worthy principle is perhaps extended *too* far.

It's instructive to note there is no consistency in how three major Hebrew New Testament translations (Hutter, Delitzsch, and Salkinson-Ginsburg[50]) render *didaskalos* and *didaskale*. At any rate, a strict *didaskalos-rabbi* equivalence is not obvious even to other skilled and knowledgeable Hebrew translators—who have not used *rabbi* quite as widely as Chouraqui. His broadened use of the term, however, intrigues the modern-day reader as she faces some of the many questions that remain, regarding our contemporary knowledge of first-century Judaism.

TOUCHED BY AN *ANGELOS*

The noun *angelos* occurs fifty-four times in the Gospels, especially in Matthew and Luke; traditionally, it has been translated in a straightforward way, as "angel."

Centuries of Christian iconography have portrayed angels as magnificent, otherworldly—and winged. Witness the pudgy *putti* of Raphael. And check out these Vatican frescoes by Melozzo da Forlì, with their heavenly minstrels:

Detail from Raphael's *Sistine Madonna*, 1513–14
From the Old Masters Picture Gallery, Dresden; image from Google Arts & Culture:
https://g.co/arts/1ZoXcZrDcM9R74fs8

Translation for Transformation

By daryl_mitchell (https://commons.wikimedia.org/wiki/File:Melozzo_da_Forl%C3%AC_Fresco_(14993275603).jpg), from Wikimedia Commons

Lost in these artistic renderings was the inherent link between *angelos* and related Greek terms, such as *angellia* (announcement, proclamation, message), *evangelion* (a formal declaration of happy or beneficial news), and the verb *angellō* (to announce, to declare, to proclaim) and its derivatives (*epangellō*, *diangellō*, etc.). *Angelos* is the Greek Septuagint's equivalent of the Hebrew *mal'āk̠*, "a messenger." The Hebrew root from which it comes conveys the notion of sending someone to bear a message; in modern terms, an *angelos* has more in common with a bike courier than with a bird, a bat or some other winged creature. As Chouraqui notes in *L'Univers de la Bible*, "the Hebrew word *malakh*...doesn't have the purely spiritual meaning that the word 'angel' later acquired."[51]

Bible readers today, conditioned by centuries of artistic representations, popular culture, and perhaps even sermons at their own churches, don't generally associate the concept of announcing or delivering a message with the word *angel*.

For many, the term is exclusively associated with heavenly figures, which doesn't take into account the passages in which *angelos* clearly means an earthly, human figure (such as the application of Malachi 3:1 to John the Baptist in Matthew 11:10, Mark 1:2, and Luke 7:27, and Luke 9:52, in which Jesus sends "messengers" [*angelous*] ahead of him). Chouraqui's compromise is to settle on the more prosaic *messenger*, which he feels captures more accurately the sense of the Greek term and its Hebrew antecedents, open to both an *earthly* and a *heavenly* interpretation according to the context.

NON-*PROPHĒTĒS* ASSOCIATION

Given the prediction/fulfillment motif that undergirds the Gospels and early Christianity, it's unsurprising the Greek noun *prophētēs* occurs eighty-six times in these four books. But instead of the expected French term *prophète*, Chouraqui has once again bucked tradition.

For many modern readers, *prophet* and *prophecy* are often equated with clairvoyance and predicting the future—rather than their biblical meanings: being an intermediary of a word received from God, an authorized interpreter of the times in the light of God's message (from the Greek preposition *pro* + *phēmi*, "to declare; make known"; or *phainō*, "to bring to light; make to appear; reveal; disclose").

Chouraqui's alternative, "inspired one" (*inspiré*) is an inspired one, considering both Old and New Testament contexts. Past generations of scholars often linked the Hebrew term for a prophet, *nābî'*, with the idea of prophetic ecstasy: an altered state of consciousness often accompanied by frenzied motion, during which apparently mystical utterances are made. Such people appear to experience a type of involuntary possession, during which their bodies and minds are temporarily occupied, ostensibly by a force external to themselves (a prime ancient example would be the role of the ancient Greek Oracle of Delphi). At any rate, more recent scholarship has tended to largely discount this linguistic association anyway, seeing *nābî'* instead as related to a root meaning "to be called, summoned, appointed." Theodor Christiaan Vriezen and A. S. van der Woude argue, for example, that "the Hebrew word employed most frequently for a prophet (*nābî'*) means a person 'called' by YHWH....Israel's prophets were thus primarily mediators and preachers of a personal experience of divine revelation."[52]

Chouraqui's poetic take on this is "someone into whom [God] has breathed" ("inspire" is from the Latin *in* + *spiro*, "to breathe into"). These people, in whom God's creative spirit was active, spoke

Translation for Transformation

not on their own, but with a unique, God-given spiritual insight. The ascription of unique spiritual insight to a "spirit" issuing from God is pre-Christian, attested already in Sirach and Wisdom:

- Sirach 48:24: "In the power of the spirit [Isaiah] saw the last things" (New Jerusalem Bible; New Revised Standard Version has "By his dauntless spirit he saw the future").
- Wisdom 7:7: "I prayed, and understanding was given me; I called on God, and the spirit of wisdom came to me."
- Wisdom 9:17: "Who has learned your counsel, unless you have given wisdom and sent your holy spirit from on high?"

It is also found in later rabbinic texts:

- Leviticus Rabbah 21:8: "Rabbi Hanina ben Hakinai… went to study Torah at Rabbi Akiba's college at Bene Berak, and stayed there thirteen years.…Rabbi Hanina did not send and did not know what was happening at his house. His wife sent him word and told him: 'Your daughter is marriageable, come and get her married.' [He said nothing to his master.] Nevertheless *Rabbi Akiba saw it by means of the Holy Spirit* and said to him: 'If anyone has a marriageable daughter, he may go and get her married.'"
- Babylonian Talmud, tractate *Berakot* 10a: "In those days was Hezekiah sick unto death. And Isaiah the prophet, son of Amoz, came to him and said unto him, Thus saith the Lord, Set thy house in order, for thou shalt die and not live, etc.…[Hezekiah] said to [Isaiah]: Why so bad? [Isaiah] replied: Because you did not try to have children. [Hezekiah] said: The reason was because *I saw by the holy spirit* that the children issuing from me would not be virtuous."

Resurrecting moribund theological vocabulary

- Babylonian Talmud, tractate *Yoma* 73b: "No priest was inquired of *who does not speak by means of the Holy Spirit* and upon whom the Divine Presence does not rest"

The idea of an *inspiré* or "inspired one" as someone who speaks with God's commission and authority seems to accord well with the idea of prophecy, in both the Old and New Testaments. Likewise, Chouraqui generally translates the verb *prophēteuō* with some form of "to be inspired" (Matthew 7:22; 11:13; 15:7; Mark 7:6; Luke 1:67; John 11:51).

Two of the more significant words in the four Gospels are "disciple" (*mathētēs*; 219 occurrences) and the less common, but equally important, technical term "apostle" (*apostolos*; ten occurrences). They are terms regularly used in Christian discourse and theological discussion, particularly in the field of ecclesiology. Neither, however, occurs in Chouraqui's Bible in the French form that would normally be expected (*disciple* or *apôtre*). Today these terms have such a "churchy" feel to them that Chouraqui felt compelled to avoid the usual translations, which suggest to readers a whole cluster of ideas extraneous to the original biblical usage.

Once again, Chouraqui's choice of terms flows from his interest in languages, and his particular sensitivity to etymology. The Latin *discipulis* (from which we get the English and French "disciple") refers to a learner, pupil, or apprentice; it's a derivative of the verb *disco*, "to learn; to acquire knowledge; to become acquainted with; to be taught" (it has no relation to the dance craze of the late 1970s and early 1980s!).[53] It's a term closely bound up with the process of education and learning. Similarly, the Greek term *mathētēs* derives from the verb *manthanō*, "to acquire information as the result of instruction, or experience, whether in an informal or formal context; to learn, to be instructed, to be taught; to come to realize; to understand."[54]

For many Christian readers today, these connotations are largely lost, and "disciple" in the New Testament comes to mean simply "a follower of Jesus." Chouraqui's alternative is a striking one; instead of "disciple," he uses the noun "adept," which is as uncommon in French as it is in English. It's an evocative choice on several levels. First, linguistically, it derives—via the term *adeptus*—from the Latin verb *adipiscor*, "to arrive at; to reach; to attain something by effort or striving." It suggests those who have successfully reached the goal of their searching, and implies a certain *struggle* or *process* of learning that has been gradually overcome. But it's also a term with a very particular history: in the Middle Ages, "adept" was used in the world of alchemy, to describe those who, after years of labor and intensive study, claimed to have discovered the Great Secret (how to turn base metals like lead into gold); it thus had the somewhat softened meaning of "someone who is completely skilled in all the secrets of their field."

Historians of religion often use the term *adept* with reference to the ancient mystery religions that were so prevalent in the Mediterranean in the centuries around the time of Jesus. An adept was someone who, through a series of initiatory stages, had penetrated into the inner, hidden mysteries of the religion, who understood its rituals, symbols, and their meaning. To be an adept implied a lengthy and intensive master-disciple relationship, gradually being led further and further into the secrets of the god or goddess (Isis-Osiris, Mithras, Serapis, Hermes, etc.)—secrets that were never to be revealed to an outsider.

Is "adept" a suitable category in which to consider discipleship as we see it described in the Gospels? On some levels, the link is an attractive one, drawing both upon the social-religious framework of the ancient Mediterranean, and upon certain aspects of intimacy and obscurity/secrecy that we see in the relationship of Jesus and those who followed him. The idea that disciples are "learners"—people who are "on the way"—and that Jesus is portrayed as (and addressed as) their Master/Teacher is accurate. But the comparison is unsatisfactory on several other levels.

First, the Gospels portray Jesus's ministry as a largely *public* matter—there is relatively little of the secrecy and exclusiveness that is normally associated with both the mystery cults and medieval alchemy. Jesus's primary message is not destined for a small, élite

Resurrecting moribund theological vocabulary

circle of "initiates"—although the Twelve *are* privy to explanations, experiences and teachings that are not provided to "the crowds." For example, in Matthew 13:10–13:

> Then the disciples came and asked him, "Why do you speak to [the crowds] in parables?" He answered, "To you it has been given to know the secrets of the kingdom of heaven, but to them it has not been given. For to those who have, more will be given, and they will have an abundance; but from those who have nothing, even what they have will be taken away. The reason I speak to them in parables is that 'seeing they do not perceive, and hearing they do not listen, nor do they understand.'"

Etymologically, *adeptus* suggests someone who "has arrived," who has attained a superior level of understanding reserved for very few. However, what we see in the Gospels, repeatedly, is a general *lack* of comprehension of many of Jesus's key teachings by many of those who hear him. Many of his more cryptic sayings would have been virtually incomprehensible in their original context, and would only make sense in retrospect, in the wake of the events of Jesus's passion, death, and resurrection. The intense master-student relationship is also lacking: the Gospels largely portray "the disciples" as a loose (and probably fluctuating) body of individuals, with minimal structure or cohesion. Finally, there seems to be little scholarly consensus about the degree to which the mystery cults had made inroads in Roman-ruled Palestine during the decades of Jesus's life. According to Everett Ferguson in his *Backgrounds of Early Christianity*:

> Although Christianity had points of contact with Stoicism, the mysteries, the Qumran community, and so on, the total worldview was often quite different....So far as we can tell, Christianity represented a new combination for its time....At the beginning of the Christian era a number of local mysteries, some of great antiquity, flourished in Greece and Asia Minor. In the first century A.D. the

only mysteries whose extension may be called universal were the mysteries of Dionysus and those of the eastern gods, especially Isis.[55]

And Norman Perrin and Dennis C. Duling note, in their book *The New Testament* (emphasis added):

> Examples of such mystery religions could be found in Greece…Asia Minor…Syria-Palestine…Persia…and Egypt. Though the mysteries had sacred shrines in these regions, many of them spread to other parts of the empire, including Rome. There is no clearly direct influence of the mysteries on early Christianity, but they shared a common environment and many non-Christians would have *perceived* Christians as members of an oriental Jewish mystery cult.[56]

Given the sparse archaeological and literary evidence from this period regarding mystery cults in Roman Palestine, and the apparent resistance of many Palestinian Jews to religious syncretism, Chouraqui's use of the noun *adept* implies a comparison between the historical Jesus and mystery cults that is doubtful, on both the levels of chronology and religious culture. Personally, I believe this choice suggests a vision of Jesus that distances him from the religious world of ancient Judaism, thus creating a distorted view of what spiritually inspired him. But the idea of the disciples as "learners" on a journey (as the Greek term suggests) is a striking one to consider; certainly, the Gospels show us the Twelve as people who are growing, learning, and developing…but who have not yet "arrived" at the fullness of their vocation.

The second key term, *apostolos* (traditionally "apostle"), is changed by Chouraqui to *envoyé* (a "sent one" or "envoy"/"ambassador"). This is a more defensible and obvious shift, with more to recommend it. Simply put, the Greek noun *apostolos* is a derivative of the verb *apostellō*, which means "to send out, often with a mandate or a mission; to cause someone to depart for a particular purpose; to send with authority or a commission." This meaning aligns well with Jewish culture and terminology at that time. Thomas F. Torrance has pointed out, in his book *Atonement: The Person and Work of Christ*:

> The Hebrew word for apostle is *shaliach*, which means a representative or ambassador sent by someone to represent them in some action or communication. "A man's *shaliach* is as himself," or in other words, as if he is the man himself, and his word and actions as though they are those of the man himself present in person. The rabbis used to speak of several of the Old Testament prophets as *sheluchim* or *shelichim*....They restricted the term to the prophets who not only spoke the word of God but were obviously authorized by certain miraculous deeds as bearers of the word of God. *Shaliach* referred to the person who speaks for God and acts for God in miraculous signs." In a certain sense, Jesus is portrayed as the *shaliach* of his Father, and the Twelve are subsequently commissioned to serve in a *shaliach* role on Jesus' behalf.[57]

The apostle is, both linguistically and in terms of his/her role, the "sent-out one" (the KJV and the RSV both render *apostolos* in John 13:16 as "he that/who is sent"). It's noteworthy that, in this same verse, the main French translations (TOB, BFC, BdeJ, Bay) all render *apostolos* as *envoyé* [envoy]; Maredsous has "messenger," as do most English versions.[58]

Unfortunately, in both French and English today, the term *apostle* has generally lost its connectedness to the idea of "sending." *Apostolic* tends to be used, either of the foundations of Christianity (such as the line in the Nicene Creed: "one, holy, catholic and *apostolic* church"), of the historical succession of bishops ("apostolic succession"), or of those who engage in active missionary outreach or community service (an "apostolic" religious community, versus a cloistered or enclosed community). Chouraqui's use of "envoy" recaptures well the original sense of sending, and reminds the reader that the "envoy" has been sent *by someone else*, and doesn't set out simply on his/her own initiative. To be "apostolic," Chouraqui seems to say, is necessarily to be outward-looking, and conscious of bearing a message from another—essential aspects of the Christian understanding of what an "apostle" is. It implies a relationship, and it entails a serious responsibility to communicate that someone's message faithfully.

The Greek expression *to pneuma hagion* is one that is found twenty-five times in the Gospels and is traditionally translated in French as *l'Esprit Saint* or *le Saint-Esprit*—the Holy Spirit.

But Chouraqui realizes that for many Christian readers—living in the wake of the trinitarian controversies and councils of the first five hundred years of Christianity—the automatic association of this term will be with one of the three persons of the Holy Trinity, as defined by more than fifteen hundred years of Christian dogma. To sidestep this lens and the theological assumptions it includes, Chouraqui chooses a less familiar—but equally valid—translation: "the sacred breath" (*le souffle sacré*). He knows that both the Hebrew word *rûaḥ* and the Greek *pneuma* can mean "breath" as well as "spirit" and "wind."

While diverging from the more traditional Christian rendering, Chouraqui's phrase has much to recommend it. First, it's a reminder that this expression is not foreign to the Hebrew Scriptures—and was not invented by Christianity: it's found in Psalm 51:11 ("your holy spirit") and Isaiah 63:10–11 ("his holy spirit"), both of which seem to express an impersonal *emanation* of God, or an extension of God's *active power*. The "spirit of the Lord" or the "spirit of God" is referred to in various other places in the Hebrew Bible, including Exodus 31:3; Numbers 24:2; 1 Samuel 10:10; Ezekiel 11:24; and elsewhere.

The expression doesn't, however, possess the more specifically *personal* quality that it will acquire in the New Testament in the preaching of Jesus (and perhaps also, later, in the Kabbalah, the classic text of Jewish mysticism).[59] Chouraqui's rendering therefore provides a subtle but helpful linguistic bridge between Testaments, allowing for, but neither presupposing nor endorsing, the connections seen by New Testament and patristic authors, and emphasizing conceptual continuity between Jewish and Christian Scriptures.[60]

Second, whereas "spirit" is an invisible and intangible concept, "breath" is a more organic, experiential image. It suggests an image of God that, while admittedly more anthropomorphic, also captures a certain intimacy and immanence (see, e.g., Genesis 2:7), avoiding some theological descriptions, often rooted in Greek philosophical categories, that have made the Godhead seem austere, distant, impenetrable, and almost aloof. The shift to using breath imagery also allows for an entirely different register of biblical associations, which are not as evident with the usual translation of "spirit."

Given Chouraqui's clear preference for the concrete over the abstract, "the sacred breath" captures a valuable, often overlooked interpretation of this expression, illuminating a richer constellation of biblical allusions with regards to this fundamental term in the Christian theological repertoire. It thus invites a more sophisticated conversation between Jews and Christians, as to the possible nuances of this term—both those they share and those they don't.

OUT WITH THE GREEK, IN WITH THE HEBREW

Today it's a commonplace of New Testament historical and theological scholarship that Jesus was born a Jew, was raised in a devout Jewish family, and remained a Jew until his death. Although scholars today question specifically *what type of Jew* Jesus was, within the constellation of Second Temple Jewish sects and movements, it's generally agreed that Jesus's lifestyle and outlook were, broadly speaking, consistent with what we know of Jewish life at that time, especially in small-town Galilee. Consequently, Chouraqui and many others today are at pains to highlight some of the ways in which Jesus's Jewishness is presented (or at least hinted at) in the Gospels. Very often, Christian translators of the New Testament, less familiar with Jewish life, theology, and interpretive traditions, have not been particularly sensitive to these issues in their work; these are religious and cultural lacunae that Chouraqui hopes to at least partly remedy in his translation. Attempting to "read between the lines" of the existing Greek text, Chouraqui asks himself, Is there a specifically Jewish or Semitic concept that might plausibly lie beneath the present Hellenistic garb?

For example, the question has often been raised of the best way to translate the Greek noun *kraspedon*, which is found (in singular or plural form) five times in the Gospels (Matthew 9:20; 14:36; 23:5; Mark 6:56; Luke 8:44), each time with reference to the garments of Jesus.

In the past, many vernacular translations have rendered this as "the edge" or "the hem" of his cloak. Chouraqui, however, sees this as an allusion to Jesus's wearing (as a devout Jewish man) of *tzitzit*, the ritual fringes or tassels that Jewish men were commanded (in Numbers 15:38 and Deuteronomy 22:12) to attach to the corners of their clothes, as a constant reminder of the covenant. In each of the five verses listed above, Chouraqui's rendering is *tzitzit*.

Is he, in fact, correct in his assumption, or is this an example of a forced interpretation for apologetic purposes? The Traduction Œcuménique de la Bible (TOB) and the French Jerusalem Bible both render this phrase as "the fringe of his robe," and the Maredsous translation has "the *houppe* [tuft; cluster; knotted part] of his robe"— all of them at least hinting at a reading in keeping with Chouraqui's. The latest edition of the New American Bible has "tassel [possibly fringe]" in Matthew 9:20, and its notes specifically reference this Jewish custom.

Such a reading is not, however, either new or novel. Already in the mid-eighteenth century, the English Baptist commentator John Gill (1697–1771), whose work is distinguished by his extensive linkages to Hebrew and rabbinic sources, confirmed this interpretation.

Resurrecting moribund theological vocabulary

In his *Exposition of the New Testament* (3 vols., 1746–48), he writes, in his comments on Matthew 9:20,

> *Touched the hem of his garment*; which was the [*tzitzit*], or *fringes*, the Jews were obliged to wear on the borders of their garments, and on it a ribband of blue; see Numb. xv, 38, Deut. xxii, 12, in both which places [the Aramaic translation] uses the word [*krospodyn*], the same with [*kraspeda*] used here, and in Mark vi, 56, and rendered *hem*. The Jews placed much sanctity in the wear and use of these fringes; and the Pharisees, who pretended to more holiness than others, enlarged them beyond their common size; but it was not on account of any particular holiness in this part of Christ's garment that induced this poor woman to touch it; but this being behind him, and more easy to be come at, she therefore laid hold of it; for it was his garment, any part of it she concluded, if she could but touch, she should have a cure. However, we learn from hence, that Christ complied with the rites of the ceremonial law in apparel, as well as in other things.[61]

More recent scholarship, both Jewish and Christian, has tended to endorse the *tzitzit* translation:

> Running like an undercurrent in Mark's narrative, obscured by the immediacy of his polemical concerns, is Jesus the traditionally religious Jew. He frequents synagogues on the Sabbath, a normatively pious practice. The ill grab hold of "the fringe of his garment" (6:56); the term, *kraspedon* in Greek, translates the Hebrew *tzitzit*.... Pious Jews would (and do) wear these; if Jesus did, too, it would be small surprise....In brief, and Mark's conscious efforts to the contrary notwithstanding, Jesus appears even in this Gospel as a recognizably observant Jew.[62]

Translation for Transformation

Ancient Jewish sources describe two distinctively Jewish items of clothing: *tzitzit* and *tefillin*. Jesus, the Pharisees, and presumably other pietists in the land of Israel wore *tzitzit* in public, tasseled fringes affixed to the four corners of one's garment in accordance with the injunctions of Numbers 15:37–41 and Deuteronomy 22:12.[63]

Jesus's connection to Judaism can be seen not only in his general comments about Torah but also in his practice of its commandments. For example, Jesus dresses like a Jew. Specifically, he wears *tzitzit*, "fringes," which the book of Numbers enjoins upon all Israelite men (and a number of Orthodox Jewish men still wear) and which can be seen today most readily in the *tallit*, or "prayer shawl," worn in the synagogue during worship....The Gospels do not shy away from the fact that Jesus wore these fringes: it is these fringes that the woman with the twelve-year hemorrhage touches in hopes of a healing (Matthew 9:20).[64]

An ancient mosaic of this scene in the Roman Catacomb of Marcellinus and Peter seems to depict precisely this detail.

The recently built church on the site of ancient Magdala includes a particularly striking mural that shows this scene, and the woman reaching out to touch the fringes of Jesus's prayer shawl (*tallit*).

Perhaps the impact of such a change on the nonspecialist reader is minimal (beyond some initial perplexity). However, by drawing attention to this small but significant detail, already contained in

From Wikimedia Commons (https://commons.wikimedia.org/wiki/File:Healing_of_a_bleeding_women_Marcellinus-Peter-Catacomb.jpg)

Resurrecting moribund theological vocabulary

the Gospels, Chouraqui both helps us to reimage the historical Jesus in light of his religious culture and enables Christians and Jews to see a concrete connection between the historical Jesus and a custom that is familiar to—and still practiced by—many modern Jews. He further reinforces this connection with a diagram and note on page 76 of this volume of his *L'Univers de la Bible*, in which he illustrates the tying of the *tzitzit*, showing them as part of a modern *tallit*, and explaining some of the numerical and mystical associations of the threads and knots.

www.magdala.org

One of the most thought-provoking examples of how intent Chouraqui is on linguistic derivations is his rendering of the Beatitudes in Matthew and Luke. It has long been acknowledged that, behind Jesus's use of the term "Blessed is/are..." (Greek *makarios/makarioi*) stands a Hebrew exclamation, *ashrei*, a form that is found forty times in the Hebrew Bible.

Translators have long grappled with the best way to appropriately express the meaning and form of this Hebrew expression: "O, the happinesses of!," "How fortunate," "How blessed," "Blessed is/are." Chouraqui focuses on the underlying verbal root, *'–sh–r*, which can mean "go straight, go on, advance." To Chouraqui, "blessedness" is a secondary, derivative meaning—in effect, the reward/consequence for the one who "walks straight" in a moral and religious sense, who "keeps to the path" as sketched out by God's law. Some scholars have even suggested that "Congratulations!" might not be too far off the mark, in terms of communicating what the Hebrew idiom means.[65]

Translation for Transformation

On this basis, the later versions of *La Bible Chouraqui* have used a radically *different* translation,[66] one that many readers admire, and others fervently detest: *En marche!*—"Rise up!" "Forward!" or "Let's get going!"—a call to arise from social marginalization and continue a journey on the proper path, the path toward a very different future, in which fortunes will be reversed by God, and sufferings will be transformed into happiness and reward. Chouraqui notes the following in *L'Univers de la Bible*:

> The first word of the Sermon on the Mount is, in most translations, the main obstacle to understanding Yeshua's message. *Makarioi*, the Greek says—"Blessed"—and this word immediately sends commentators off on the wrong track. The "Beatitudes" are assumed to be something that should be possessed from the outset, whereas they will only be fully realized in the kingdom of *Adonai*. And Jesus did not say *makarioi*, but *ashrei* (see Psalm 1:1), an exclamation…from the root *ashar* which implies, not the idea of a vague and essentially hedonistic happiness, but the idea of uprightness, *yashar*—the uprightness of the person who is walking on a path clear of obstacles—the path that leads toward Adonai.[67]

Linguist and theologian Erasmo Leiva-Merikakis interprets Chouraqui's choice this way:

> The Hebrew "subtext" of the Gospel also adds a valuable dimension to the meaning of [*makarios*]. The Jewish translator of the New Testament Andre Chouraqui suggests that the Hebrew equivalent…(*ashrei*) indicates the thrill of the wayfarer who is about to reach his goal, in other words, the joy of the pilgrim who never halts in his movement toward the sanctuary of the heavenly homeland where God his Father awaits him. Chouraqui therefore translates [*makarios*] as "underway" or "forward," thus keynoting movement toward the good goal and the

rejoicing that fills the pilgrim at being sure that he will reach God by this road and no other. Here again, it seems that the traditional Spanish translation *bienaventurado* has always conveyed this sense. Those who live according to the desires of the Lord's Heart as here expressed have undertaken the *buena aventura* or "good adventure": they hasten toward the God who calls them and leave everything else behind.[68]

Jean-Marie de Bourqueney, a French theologian and pastor, says that Chouraqui's translation "recovers somewhat the sense of this 'jubilescence.'…Our existence is always a *becoming*, and thus a movement forward.…Life is about continuing to keep walking."[69] If that *is*, indeed, inherent in the biblical understanding of blessedness, then Chouraqui's rendering can help us to recapture some of the joyful forward movement of life when lived according to God's plan.

In his quest to refresh and renew biblical language, sometimes Chouraqui deliberately tampers with a fixed expression that has become proverbial. In Matthew 6:28, Jesus employs the Greek expression *ta krina tou agrou* (traditionally, "the lilies of the field"), and the floral term is partially reprised in Luke 12:27 ("Consider the lilies, how they grow"). Chouraqui, however, renders the Greek *krina* in Matthew with "the *amaryllises* of the field." A reader even slightly familiar with the phrase as it has been adopted into colloquial French or English is left puzzling over the unexpected choice of the amaryllis over the lily. Still more puzzling is that Chouraqui, for unspecified reasons, translates the Lucan occurrence as "Observe the lilies and their growth"! Although *krinon* occurs only twice in the entire New Testament, it's treated differently in each passage, although the literary and theological parallels between them seem clear.

Has Chouraqui made this choice simply to be provocative, mischievous…or pedantic? What is the logic that undergirds this deviation from such a familiar phrasing? Late twentieth-century commentators and translators have tended to take a more agnostic approach when it comes to specifying the exact strain of flowers referred to in biblical texts. While the RSV/NRSV and Maredsous versions continue to use the familiar "*lilies* of the field," many other contemporary versions clearly prefer a less exact rendering:

> NAB: "Learn from the way the wild flowers grow."
>
> NET Bible: "Think about how the flowers of the field grow."
>
> NJB: "Think of the flowers growing in the fields."
>
> Bible en français courant: "Observe how the flowers of the fields grow."

Trying to establish with precision the botanical equivalents of ancient flora, especially based on vague or incidental comments like this, is a nearly impossible task. Often, the descriptions are insufficient for certainty, or are part of metaphors whose goal is other than scientific taxonomy.

As several commentators point out, part of the difficulty lies in matching a specific plant with the characteristics given in the Bible (Is it, in fact, a *wildflower* [vs. a cultivated garden variety], and a species native to Israel? Does its habitat as described match up with what we know from botany? The biblical *šušan* is said to bloom in the valleys, among brambles, and in the meadowlands where shepherds might pasture their sheep [Song of Solomon 2:1, 16]). These descriptions—and the question of how much scientific weight is to be attributed to them—have led to generations of debate among exegetes and scholars of the floral world:

> The most frequently mentioned specific flowers are traditionally translated "lily" [Heb *šušan*] and "rose" [Heb *ḥavatzelet*]....Students of Palestinian botany tell us that neither of these is probably the correct translation, however. The lily familiar to most readers, the white or "Easter" lily (*Lilium candidum*), grows in remote regions of Israel, but does not fit the description attributed to it in

Resurrecting moribund theological vocabulary

the biblical text....Many commentators now assume, for example, that the phrase "lilies of the field" means any of the showy, attractive flowers that burst forth in glorious profusion in the springtime on the plains, pastures and hills of the Carmel and Sharon regions....These flowers include ranunculus, anemone, cyclamen, tulip, hyacinth, narcissus, crocus, iris and orchid. Any reference to lilies or roses in the following discussion could therefore just as easily be substituted with any of those species, or could be understood to be making a generic reference to flowers.[70]

Ta krina tou agrou, customarily translated as "the lilies of the field," does not refer specifically to the *šušannîm* [the usual Hebrew term for lilies]...but, more generally, to "wild flowers," and perhaps to the *anemone coronaria* which, on account of its bright and varied colors, would serve as a good point of comparison for the glory of Solomon's royal purple [robes].[71]

To resolve this difficulty of identification, it is important to recall that, for the ancients...the names of plants did not always have a precise definition. And so it was that, for the Greeks, even if a word had an agreed-upon meaning, and designated the white lily (although sometimes it was also used of the narcissus!), the most frequently used word...has a more generic meaning, and also includes the orange-tinged lily and several other species of plants....Similarly, among speakers of Semitic languages, the word *šušan* did not have a precise definition....The Arabic term *susan* includes not only the lily, but...also the *Pancratium Maritimum* [sea daffodil] or the Matthiola lily [a family that includes nearly 50 species of flowers]....The term [in Arabic] therefore has quite a bit of elasticity. It was probably the same for the Hebrew word *šušan*; it could include various species of plants, from the families of lilies, irises, amaryllises, *fritillaria*, etc., just as, in everyday language, we call various flowers by the name of lily.[72]

As regards the flower described as the *krinon*, there appear to be three schools of thought today:

1. that a white, conical flower with petals is envisaged, either identical to or similar to the familiar Easter lily;

2. that the reference in Matthew 6:28, comparing this flower and the glory of Solomon's vesture, is to be taken in terms of its *color*, which would suggest a crimson or purple flower, similar to the ancient purple favored by royalty; or

3. that *no specific flower* is intended, and *ta krina tou agrou* is simply a vivid figure of speech, referring to the beauty, rich color, and variety of spring wildflowers; it would therefore be merely a generic or collective term, and no particular species should be sought out (see the biblical versions cited above, for example).

Traditionally, what has been pointed out to generations of pilgrims and students as Jesus's "lily of the field" is the *anemone coronaria* (windflower), a brilliant crimson flower that could seem to suggest the reddish-purple of imperial robes; others have argued in favor of the Chalcedon lily (*Lilium chalcedonicum*), a particularly striking variety of scarlet flower. Both seem to presume that the point of reference for Jesus's allusion is the rich, regal *color* of the blossom in question.

Under Matthew 6:28 in *L'Univers de la Bible* (64), Chouraqui gives us a hint as to his own conclusions, with this note: "amaryllis, or *Pancratium*, the *ḥavatzelet* of Isaiah 35:1 and Song 2:1."

While Chouraqui is apparently conversant with the typical flora of modern Israel, it's also possible that the deciding factor for him in his choice of "amaryllis, or *Pancratium*" was, in fact, his familiarity with the related Arabic term, as outlined in Vigouroux's *Dictionnaire de la Bible*, above. In any case, the considerable scholarly debate about the particular floral species referred to by Jesus—or whether it's *a particular species* at all—seems to suggest that Chouraqui's rendering, as unusual as it is, falls well within the spectrum of acceptable hypotheses, based on his own particular linguistic and/or botanical deductions.

Interestingly, Chouraqui's unorthodox determination is reminiscent of a similar episode fifteen hundred years earlier, in which the misidentification of a biblical plant provoked liturgical chaos. St. Jerome, in the process of translating the Vulgate, had rendered the Hebrew *qiqayon*—the plant God caused to grow to shelter Jonah in Jonah 4:6 (and found *only* in Jonah 4)—by the Latin *hedera* (ivy). This innovative translation—based on Jerome's own inquiries and deductions—broke with older translations (including the Septuagint) that understood the plant as a gourd or castor-oil plant. St. Augustine, in his *Letter 72*, writes to Jerome, chastising him for this shocking innovation, which had apparently spurred a near-riot in the diocese of Oea when initially read aloud in the liturgy:

> There was a certain brother bishop of ours who decided to read your translation in the church over which he presided, and he caused a sensation by some passage from the Prophet Jonas, which was very different from the version enshrined in the memory and hearing of all, and sung for so many generations. There was such a disturbance made among the people by the Greeks arguing and stirring up passions with the charge of falsity, that the bishop...was forced to call on the testimony of the Jews. Was it through ignorance or malice that they answered that what the Greeks and Latins said and maintained was found in the Hebrew texts? To make a long story short, the man was forced to correct an apparently wrong statement, not wishing to run the great risk of remaining without a flock. After this, it seems to us that you, also, among

others, can be wrong, and you see the sort of thing that can happen.[73]

Having made his home in Israel for several decades, Chouraqui possessed a certain lived experience of the land, its flora, and fauna that he believed could help him as a translator, informing his renderings in a way that translators outside the Holy Land often would not have access to. Knowing the Holy Land firsthand and intimately (as he did) could be an asset in translating the Bible—and Chouraqui believed that it was.

בֶּן בַּג בַּג אוֹמֵר, הֲפֹךְ בָּהּ וַהֲפֹךְ בָּהּ, דְּכֹלָּא בָהּ. וּבָהּ תֶּחֱזֵי, וְסִיב
וּבְלֵה בָהּ, וּמִנַּהּ לֹא תָזוּעַ, שֶׁאֵין לְךָ מִדָּה טוֹבָה הֵימֶנָּה:

Ben Bag-Bag used to say: Turn it [the text of the Scripture] and turn it again, for everything is contained in it. Contemplate it, and grow old and gray (studying it) and do not abandon it, for you have no better occupation than this.

(Mishnah, tractate *Pirqe Avot* 5:22)

5

COGNATES, FORMAL EQUIVALENCE, AND THE TWO JERUSALEMS

CHOURAQUI'S RENDERING OF HEBREW DUAL AND PLURAL FORMS

One of the consequences of Chouraqui's decision to employ the wide range of Hebrew proper names and theological terms (which we explored in the last chapter) is that he must then unpack certain aspects of these terms and their forms. These often differ from French and English, and may frequently be of exegetical or linguistic interest, but will not be immediately obvious to someone who has not studied biblical languages.[74]

One of the ways in which Chouraqui achieves this is quite novel: in the case of both the Hebrew masculine plural and dual suffixes (*-im*, *-ayim*), Chouraqui often adds an additional *s* to his transliteration to signal to his readers that the foreign word in front of him or her is, in fact, indicative of "more than one." To someone already familiar with Hebrew, this can come across as a linguistic oddity, adding a (French) plural suffix where one is already present as part of the word itself. However, the average reader of Chouraqui's work is unlikely to intuit that *Peroushim* (Pharisees) is, in fact, the plural form of *Peroush*, that

Sopherim (scribes) is the plural of *sopher*, or that *Shomronîm* (Samaritans) pluralizes *Shomroni*; these therefore become *Peroushîms*, *Sopherîms*, and *Shomronîms*, respectively. Once one grasps the logic of Chouraqui's project, this morphological signal is understandable, if perhaps unorthodox. Chouraqui is attempting to guide his readers into appreciating some of the particularities of Hebrew, without a formal course in grammar. He is trying to point to details that might be worthy of further investigation—or can at least make the reader pause and ask questions about what is going on.

What is more striking—and more interesting—both linguistically and theologically, is Chouraqui's decision to indicate the plural of certain more unusual terms, such as *Elohim*s, a very common word for "God" in Hebrew, but one that is—at least on the level of its morphological form—*plural*.

Scholars have traditionally characterized this as a "plural of majesty/excellence/intensity" (but have translated it as *singular*, because it is most frequently accompanied by a singular verb).[75] Chouraqui seems to see this procedure as something of a sneaky scholarly evasion, a refusal to allow the reader to grapple for himself or herself with the implications of these anomalous grammatical forms, which have intrigued and troubled interpreters—both Jewish and Christian—for centuries. He would rather be more transparent about the problem, and then allow his readers to think about the possible answers and draw their own conclusions. Chouraqui has a profound respect for his readers, and he believes that it's better to present ambiguities in the text in a forthright way, rather than "papering over" them in a way that can seem paternalistic or condescending, as an effort to avoid awkward discussions. In its own way, it represents an effort to take certain aspects of biblical scholarship out of the hands of the professional guilds alone, and make them available to laypeople—in a sense, to "democratize" somewhat the process of studying and interpreting the Bible.

YERUSHALAYIM

Why is it, for example, that the name of Jerusalem takes a specifically (and unexpectedly) *dual* form in Hebrew, as *Yerushal***ayim**

Cognates, formal equivalence, and the two Jerusalems

(for Chouraqui, *Yerushalayim***s**)? Are there, in fact, *two* Jerusalems? Jewish and Christian commentators have traditionally explained this as a reference to the "earthly/present" city of Jerusalem (*Yerushalayim shel mattah*, "Jerusalem of below"), and the "heavenly/future" city of Jerusalem (*Yerushalayim shel ma'alah*, "Jerusalem of above")—the Holy City in its eschatological perfection, in the presence of God:

> Rabbi Nahman said to Rabbi Isaac: What is the meaning of the scriptural verse, *The Holy One is in your midst, and I will not come into the city?* [Hosea 11:9]….He replied: Thus said Rabbi Yohanan: The Holy One, blessed be He, said, "I will not enter the heavenly Jerusalem until I can enter the earthly Jerusalem." Is there then a heavenly Jerusalem? Yes; for it is written, *Jerusalem, you are built as a city that is bound firmly together*. (Psalms 122:3)[76]

Drawing upon the notes on tractate *Ta'anit* 5a in the Soncino edition of the Talmud, we can see that Rabbi Yohanan is playing here with the Hebrew word *sheḥubarah* (bound together), which is linguistically related to the Hebrew word *ḥaver* (companion, associate, a person with whom you are united), to conclude that the terrestrial Jerusalem has a companion (or counterpart) in heaven. This heavenly-earthly Jerusalem dichotomy would become a significant theme in patristic commentaries and preaching. Justin Martyr, Origen, and Augustine are among the many fathers of the Church who later develop this strand of allegorical and symbolic interpretation, providing rich inspiration for Christian spirituality, liturgy, and architecture.

Although the notion of the two Jerusalems is developed in greater depth in Talmudic and later Jewish writings, it seems clear the concept was already familiar in the first half of the first century since it's drawn upon by Paul in his letter to the Galatians (48–56 CE), and in the anonymous Epistle to the Hebrews (possibly the last third of the first century CE):

> But the other woman corresponds to *the Jerusalem above*; she is free, and she is our mother. (Galatians 4:26)

> But you have come to Mount Zion and to the city of the living God, *the heavenly Jerusalem*, and to innumerable angels in festal gathering, and to the assembly of the first-born who are enrolled in heaven, and to God the judge of all, and to the spirits of the righteous made perfect. (Hebrews 12:22–23)

The idea of the "heavenly Jerusalem," waiting in God's presence to be revealed at the end of the age, in the Messianic Era, is also a central motif of the book of Revelation:

> I saw the holy city, *the new Jerusalem, coming down out of heaven from God*, prepared as a bride adorned for her husband. And I heard a loud voice from the throne saying, "See, the home of God is among mortals. He will dwell with them; they will be his peoples, and God himself will be with them." (Revelation 21:2–3)

It is precisely this ancient tradition—which Chouraqui wishes to evoke and expose to his nonspecialist readers—that lies behind his emphasis on highlighting this "duality" of Jerusalem. In these contexts, his goal is simply to point out this intriguing linguistic anomaly, without meaning to impose a specific linguistic or theological interpretation upon it. Is the answer as mundane as some have suggested: a dual form to reflect the upper and lower parts of the ancient city, just as the dual form for Egypt, *Mitzrayim*, probably corresponds to the two kingdoms of Upper and Lower Egypt? Or is there is a *further richness*—historical, theological, mystical—concealed in this dual form? Chouraqui's version invites his readers to grapple with possible reasons and their implications in a way not possible with other translations. In a world in which many Christians today are quite theologically sophisticated, Chouraqui's choice is respectful of adult learners, allowing them to draw their own (newly informed) conclusions. He challenges us to think about the meaning of the Scriptures in new and enlightening ways—and he signals some of the intriguing interpretive avenues that Jews and Christians have pursued over the last two thousand years.[77]

THE SEMITIC LINKING OF RELATED VERBS AND NOUNS

A common feature of biblical Hebrew and Greek is the use, as direct objects, of nouns linguistically linked to the transitive verb they complete.

In linguistic terms, the noun in such a construction is known as a cognate object or cognate accusative. From the Latin *cognatus*, "cognate" means "growing out of the same ancestry or origins; a blood relative." Linguistic cognates are words that, because they share common linguistic roots, are also closely linked in meaning, and thus amplify or reflect upon one another. The use of cognate objects in ancient biblical contexts generally intends to emphasize or heighten the associated verb, given that adverbs were not as plentiful in biblical Hebrew.

Showtune aficionados who've seen the stage production or movie of *Les Misérables* will remember the character Fantine singing the melancholy "I Dreamed a Dream"—a perfect example of a cognate accusative. Fantine shares her intensity of dream experience with Joseph in Genesis 37:5, who also "dreamed a dream." Other biblical examples include Genesis 8:20 ("He offered up offerings-up") and Exodus 32:32 ("You have sinned a great sin").

From the perspective of many translators who follow more of a dynamic-equivalence model, reproducing cognate objects may seem inelegant or clunky. Though there is a place for cognate accusatives as part of a rhetorical flourish or an idiomatic expression, they have often been avoided in modern biblical translation, where such repetition is often frowned upon. A classic example of this is Mark 4:41, which in Greek includes the phrase *ephobēthēsan phobon megan*—"they feared a great fear" (note the repetition of the *-phob-* cluster of letters). Many translations render this using an adverb or adverbial phrase. Others incorporate the sense of the direct object in an emotionally strengthened verb. Let's have a closer look at the strategies used by various translations in rendering this verse:

Translation for Transformation

Mark 4:41 ἐφοβήθησαν φόβον μέγαν (ephobēthēsan phobon megan)	
New Revised Standard Version/New American Bible	"They were filled with great awe"
New Jerusalem Bible/Common English Bible	"[They were] overcome with awe"
New International Version	"They were terrified"
Good News Translation	"They were terribly afraid"
Contemporary English Version	"They were more afraid than ever"
King James/Douay-Rheims versions	"They feared exceedingly"

When faced with a Greek phrase that involves repetition of similar words close together, all these translations have chosen other strategies to avoid this since the repetition may sound odd to many English speakers. But Chouraqui believes it's important to preserve this distinctive structure—beloved by ancient Hebrew authors, but also familiar in Hebrew-influenced Greek—as another way to recapture the "Semitic voice" of Jesus and the Gospels. So, he translates this phrase literally: "they trembled with great trembling."

Not only does Chouraqui not eliminate or avoid the cognate accusative, he brings it to the fore, for the benefit of readers who might not otherwise be aware of the subtle but important wordplay at work here. Throughout his translation of the Gospels, Chouraqui generally favors the reproduction of cognate forms. In the examples below (in which the Greek cognate elements that are shared are underlined), we see that Chouraqui usually goes much further than a comparable modern translation when it comes to adherence to the ancient text:

Matthew 2:10 ἐχάρησαν χαρὰν μεγάλην (echarēsan charan megalēn)	
Chouraqui Bible:	"They rejoiced with a great joy"
New Revised Standard Version	"They were overwhelmed with joy"

Cognates, Formal Equivalence, and the Two Jerusalems

Contemporary English Version	"They were thrilled and excited"
International Standard Version	"They were ecstatic with joy"
Weymouth New Testament	"The sight filled them with intense joy"
Matthew 9:16 οὐδεὶς δὲ ἐπιβάλλει ἐπίβλημα ῥάκους (oudeis de epiballei epiblēma rakous)	
Chouraqui Bible	"No one patches with an unshrunk patch"
New Revised Standard Version	"No one sews a piece of unshrunk cloth"
New English Translation (NET Bible)	"No one sews a patch of unshrunk cloth"
Mark 10:38 τὸ βάπτισμα ὃ ἐγὼ βαπτίζομαι βαπτιθῆναι (to baptisma ho egō baptizomai baptithēnai)	
Chouraqui Bible	"Be immersed with the immersion with which I am going to be immersed"
New Revised Standard Version	"Be baptized with the baptism that I am baptized with"
Berean Study Bible	"Be baptized with the baptism I will undergo"
Luke 11:46 φορτίζετε τοὺς ἀνθρώπους φορτία δυσβάστακτα (phortizete tous anthrōpous phortia dysbastakta)	
Chouraqui Bible	"You burden people with difficult burdens"
New Revised Standard Version	"You load people with burdens hard to bear"
Christian Study Bible	"You load people with burdens that are hard to carry"
Knox Bible	"Loading men with packs too heavy to be borne"
John 7:24 τὴν δικαίαν κρίσιν κρίνετε (tēn dikaian krisin krinete)	
Chouraqui Bible	"Judge with a righteous judgement"
New Revised Standard Version	"Judge with right judgment"
New American Bible	"Judge justly"

Table continued

| Jerusalem Bible | "Let your judgement be according to what is right" |

There are also examples of other related cognate forms that function in much the same way, reinforcing or intensifying the strength of the related verb:

Mark 3:28
αἱ βλασφημίαι ὅσα ἐὰν βλασφημήσωσιν
(hai <u>blasphēm</u>iai hosa ean <u>blasphēm</u>ēsōsin)

Chouraqui Bible	"All the blasphemies with which they blaspheme"
New Revised Standard Version	"Whatever blasphemies they utter"
Jerusalem Bible	"All their blasphemies"
Goodspeed translation	"All the abusive things they say"
Holman Christian Standard Bible	"Whatever blasphemies they may blaspheme"

Luke 22:15
ἐπιθυμίᾳ ἐπεθύμησα
(<u>epithum</u>ia <u>epethum</u>ēsa)

Chouraqui Bible	"I have desired with desire"
New Revised Standard Version/New American Bible	"I have eagerly desired"
English Revised Version	"With desire I have desired"
Jerusalem Bible	"I have longed"
Knox Bible	"I have longed and longed"

John 3:29
χαρᾷ χαίρει
(<u>char</u>a <u>chair</u>ei)

Chouraqui Bible	"Is cherished with cherishing"[78]
New Revised Standard Version/New American Bible	"Rejoices greatly"
Berean Literal Bible	"Rejoices with joy"
International Standard Version	"Is overjoyed"

Cognates, formal equivalence, and the two Jerusalems

John 17:26
ἡ ἀγάπη ἣν ἠγάπησάς με
(hē <u>agapē</u> hēn <u>ēgapē</u>sas me)

Chouraqui Bible	"The love with which you love (or: have loved) me"
New Revised Standard Version	"The love with which you have loved me"
Goodspeed translation	"The love which you have had for me"
Knox translation	"The love thou hast bestowed upon me"

Chouraqui's approach to cognate forms—which play on both the levels of meaning and sound—is a distinguishing mark of his translational work, and highlights both his keen interest in linguistic associations, but also his attentiveness to the esthetics, literary artistry, and oral quality of the text as he translates it. He is clearly laboring to make certain aspects of the Greek text (and the underlying Hebraic thinking) as "transparent" as he can in his work. In this, he is a worthy successor to the Buber-Rosenzweig tradition in German, an ideological contender alongside linguist and translator Henri Meschonnic in French, and a precursor of Everett Fox's later English edition of the Torah.

THE FUTURE TENSE USED AS A COMMAND

Without getting into the complexities of Hebrew grammar, the Hebrew imperfect tense (which overlaps considerably with the English *future* tense) is often used to express a command: "You shall (or shall not) do X" frequently *means* "Do (or don't do) X!" This is particularly noticeable in the Ten Commandments. For example: "You shall have no other gods before me" (Exodus 20:3) or "You shall not bow down to them or worship [idols]" (v. 5).

Taken literally, these pronouncements *can* sound like predictions for the future, but it's clear they are *not really future-tense verbs*. Our long familiarity with "Bible English" means that we instinctively understand them as *commands*, even when English grammar might suggest otherwise: "Have no other gods before me!" or "Do not bow to them or worship them!"

This is a feature that scholars often notice in the Greek New Testament, where it is often likely to be a carryover from Semitic usage. Chouraqui is aware of that nuance, and he generally translates those "imperatival futures" as the command that is intended:

Matthew 1:21 καὶ καλέσεις τὸ ὄνομα αὐτοῦ Ἰησοῦν (kai kaleseis to onoma autou Iēsoun)	
Chouraqui Bible	"Cry out his name: Yeshua'!"
NET Bible	"You will name him Jesus"
English Standard Version	"You shall call his name Jesus"
Jerusalem Bible	"You must name him Jesus"

Matthew 5:48 Ἔσεσθε οὖν ὑμεῖς τέλειοι (Esesthe oun hymeis teleioi)	
Chouraqui Bible	"Be upright, as your Father of the heavens is upright"
French Jerusalem Bible	"You shall be perfect, just as your heavenly Father is perfect"
New American Bible	"Be perfect, just as your heavenly Father is perfect"
Berean Literal Bible	"You shall be perfect, therefore, as your Heavenly Father is perfect"

Matthew 19:18 Οὐ φονεύσεις, Οὐ μοιχεύσεις, Οὐ κλέψεις, Οὐ ψευδομαρτυρήσεις (Ou phoneuseis, ou moicheuseis, ou klepseis, ou pseudomartyrēseis)	
Chouraqui Bible	"Do not assassinate; do not adulter; do not steal; do not respond as a lying witness"
New Revised Standard Version	"You shall not murder; You shall not commit adultery; You shall not steal; You shall not bear false witness"

Cognates, formal equivalence, and the two Jerusalems

English Standard Version	"You shall not murder, You shall not commit adultery, You shall not steal, You shall not bear false witness"
Jerusalem Bible	"You must not kill. You must not commit adultery. You must not bring false witness."
New English Translation (NET Bible)	"Do not murder, do not commit adultery, do not steal, do not give false testimony"

Luke 21:19
ἐν τῇ ὑπομονῇ ὑμῶν κτήσασθε τὰς ψυχὰς ὑμῶν
(en tē hypomonē hymōn ktēsasthe tas psychas hymōn)

Chouraqui Bible	"Master your own self through endurance"
New Revised Standard Version	"By your endurance you will gain your souls"
Holman Christian Standard Bible	"By your endurance gain your lives"
New American Bible	"By your perseverance you will secure your lives"

Matthew 4:7
Οὐκ ἐκπειράσεις κύριον τὸν θεόν σου
(Ouk ekpeiraseis kyrion ton theon sou)

Chouraqui Bible	"Do not test Y$^{\text{ADONAI}}_{\text{H W}}$H !"[79]
New American Bible	"You shall not put the Lord, your God, to the test"
Holman Christian Standard Bible	"Do not test the Lord your God"
Jerusalem Bible	"You must not put the Lord your God to the test"

Contrast these, however, with the following examples where, surprisingly, Chouraqui doesn't render the imperatival force of the future tense:

Matthew 21:3
ἐρεῖτε ὅτι Ὁ κύριος αὐτῶν χρείαν ἔχει
(ereite hoti ho kyrios autōn chreian echei)

Chouraqui Bible	"You shall say, 'The Lord needs them'" (not "Say: 'The Lord...'")
English Standard Version	"You shall say, 'The Lord needs them'"

Table continued

Translation for Transformation

Berean Study Bible	"Tell him that the Lord needs them"
New American Bible	"Reply, 'The master has need of them'"

Mark 12:30
καὶ ἀγαπήσεις κύριον τὸν θεόν σου ἐξ ὅλης τῆς καρδίας σου
(kai agapēseis kyrion ton theon sou ex holēs tēs kardias sou)

Chouraqui Bible	"You shall love your Elohims with all your heart" (not "Love the Lord…")
New Revised Standard Version/New American Bible	"You shall love the Lord your God with all your heart"
Berean Study Bible	"Love the Lord your God with all your heart"
Jerusalem Bible	"You must love the Lord your God with all your heart"

וְהַמַּשְׂכִּלִים יַזְהִרוּ כְּזֹהַר הָרָקִיעַ וּמַצְדִּיקֵי הָרַבִּים כַּכּוֹכָבִים לְעוֹלָם וָעֶד:

Those who are wise shall shine like the brightness of the sky, and those who lead many to righteousness, like the stars for ever and ever.

(Daniel 12:3)

6

A RICH, ICONOCLASTIC LEGACY

André Chouraqui was a man of vision and of conviction. Imaginative, creative, and intellectually curious, he left his imprint on many domains, including politics, religion, and culture. But it was his biblical translations that brought him to the attention of a much wider francophone readership, demonstrating a strikingly different model of how ancient texts could—or *should*—be translated.

To deliberately overturn centuries of literary and theological custom was an act of daring. Some critics have rejected Chouraqui as an interloper, defying the canons of acceptable French, creating an uncomfortable, pedantic Bible unsuitable for devotional or liturgical use. They say his strange hybrid language obscures more than it illuminates, and that his claims for its accuracy and cultural insight are exaggerated.

But these critics seem to be in the minority. The popularity of the *Chouraqui Bible* in the past five decades, among Jews, Christians, and even the nonreligious, demonstrates that it is a version whose raw power and "decalcified" phrasings revive the Bible, liberating it from the straitjackets of some institutional interpretations. At a time when many people describe themselves as "spiritual, but not religious," there is an obvious interest in a Bible that is not beholden to denominational interests, which can dispense with traditional theological terminology, and can suggest new ways of reading very old texts.

It is, in many senses, a pioneering effort (like the Buber-Rosenzweig German version and the English Torah of Everett Fox), and it shares both the virtues and the shortcomings of many pioneering works. Especially in such a massive work, undertaken by a single individual, a certain amount of ambivalence and debate is to be expected—and even Chouraqui's many devotees do not always share *all* his working assumptions or methods.

What many people *do* admire about Chouraqui is his breadth of knowledge and study, his willingness to experiment, his refusal to "dumb down" some of the more challenging aspects of his work, and his undeniable commitment to interfaith relationships.

I believe that the specific richness of André Chouraqui's work lies in its powers of reconciliation: religious faith with scientific inquiry; beauty with accuracy; antiquity with modernity; East with West; Jewish with Christian. The ability to achieve all of this has its foundation in the specificity of Chouraqui's religious, historical, geographical, and cultural vantage point. In the next section of this book, I'd like to broaden our understanding of his work by illuminating how it intersects with his life experience, and the particular historical moments within which his vision, and his passion, were forged.

The nineteenth-century Scottish historian Thomas Carlyle (1795–1881) famously proposed the "great men" theory of history, according to which history is largely an account of the lives of outstanding individuals whose words and actions changed the course of human affairs. Today, a more sociological school of historical analysis emphasizes equally the character of remarkable individuals, the sociocultural factors that favored their success, and the cardinal or "pregnant" moments of history in which they lived, as more accurately reflecting how world events are shaped. Where one or the other factor is lacking, prophetic voices fall upon deaf ears, and the potential for change yields only mockery, frustration, disappointment, and apathy. When, however, the *right person* lives at the *right time*, when the right ideas meet with fertile circumstances, the results can be revolutionary, and the space of a few years can turn historical probability on its head. I believe that it is that unique intersection—of a singularly remarkable individual and a "pregnant" historical period—that makes André Chouraqui's story so fascinating and significant.

At the start of the twentieth century, very few people could have predicted the dramatic transformation that would begin to take place in Jewish-Christian relations. Almost since the beginning of the Common Era, it seemed that Christianity and Judaism had been locked in an unending theological duel. Christians saw the Jews as recalcitrant, stubbornly refusing to acknowledge the truth and consequences of the Messiah's coming. The Jews, for their part, maintained that Christ was either a false or misled messianic figure, that the Church had misunderstood Hebrew prophecies applied to him, and that attributing divinity to him contradicted the fundamental unity of God.

Despite centuries of oppression, exclusion, and violence in Christian lands, Jews in Europe and North America clung tenaciously to their ancestral faith, its commandments, and rituals. To the degree that they even *encountered* Jews, Christians were likely to regard them with a blend of curiosity, suspicion, and disdain, convinced that, since the advent of Christianity, traditional Jews were little more than "theological dinosaurs," whose raison d'être had ceased to exist centuries earlier, and whose continued presence was quaint at best, and provocative at worst.

Of course, there had been some limited efforts to try and, if not *bridge*, then at least *narrow* that chasm. In January 1904, Theodor Herzl, the founding father of the Zionist movement, had come to speak to Pope Pius X in Rome, asking his support for a Jewish homeland in the land of Israel (still part of the Ottoman Empire at the time). Despite the pope's kind manner, his words left no room for doubt:

> We cannot give approval to this movement. We cannot prevent the Jews from going to Jerusalem—but we could never sanction it. The soil of Jerusalem, if it was not always sacred, has been sanctified by the life of Jesus

Christ....The Jews have not recognized our Lord, therefore we cannot recognize the Jewish people....If you come to Palestine and settle your people there, we shall have churches and priests ready to baptize all of you.[80]

In 1926, while Chouraqui was still just a child, an international group called the Opus sacerdotale Amici Israel (The Clerical Association of Friends of Israel) had been established in the Catholic Church. Its purpose? To try and reform some of the more harsh liturgical references to the Jews, to foster greater respect and understanding of Judaism among the Catholic clergy—and to pray for the conversion of the Jews. At its height, it included more than two thousand priests, nearly three hundred bishops, and nineteen cardinals. But two years later, the Friends of Israel was suppressed by order of the Vatican. Its crime? It had been *too* pro-Jewish, and its message seemed to call into question a centuries-old interpretation of how Christianity has replaced Judaism as God's chosen people. Its "manner of acting and thinking [was] contrary to the opinion and spirit of the Church, to the thinking of the Holy Fathers, and to the very liturgy."[81]

Two important footnotes in modern theological history...but they certainly did not seem to bode well for any improvement of relations between Jews and Christians. It looked as if those two religions were doomed to perpetual tension, misunderstanding, and distance. A hostility *that* old and *that* deeply rooted could never change...or *could* it? A century later, things looked very, very different. And part of the change began with a boy born to a Jewish family in colonial Algeria.

SECTION 2

UNE VIE TRÈS PLEINE

עַל שְׁלֹשָׁה דְבָרִים הָעוֹלָם עוֹמֵד: עַל הַתּוֹרָה, וְעַל הָעֲבוֹדָה, וְעַל גְּמִילוּת חֲסָדִים.
There are three pillars on which the world stands: on Torah, on service of God, and on acts of compassion.

(Mishnah, tractate *Pirqe Avot* 1:2)

7

A MAN OF THREE WORLDS

André Chouraqui lived at the confluence of several key events and trends that shaped the history, politics, and religion of the twentieth century:

- the French colonial enterprise in North Africa;
- the rise to power of the National Socialists in Germany;
- the outbreak of the Second World War;
- the brutal Nazi occupation of much of Europe, including the industrialized slaughter of six million European Jews;
- the rebirth of Israel as a political entity; and
- a radical rethinking of Christian attitudes toward Judaism, in an era of repentance, renewal, and interreligious outreach.

Not only did these events, experiences, and trends leave a powerful mark on him as a man and as a translator, but they created an atmosphere that both favored his initiatives and enabled them to become widely known and discussed. His contributions to interfaith dialogue, politics, and literature are inextricably bound with the nine decades (1917 to 2007) in which he lived. As one of the most knowledgeable scholars of Chouraqui's work, Dr. Cyril Aslanov, wrote,

> We must not overlook the subjective facts of the translator's biography.... In the particular case of André Chouraqui, and his translations of the Bible and the Qur'an, we would be mistaken if we neglected certain noteworthy aspects of his life story. For his intended goal—bringing French biblical translations closer to their ancient Semitic context—is inseparable from Chouraqui's rootedness in the heart of three cultures: the Sephardic Jewish culture of North Africa...the French culture, of which André Chouraqui is such a distinguished representative...and, finally, Hebrew-speaking Israeli culture....Without question, it is the interrelationship of these three cultural horizons which allows us to understand the revolutionary specificity of André Chouraqui's translation of the Bible.[82]

Another scholar of his work, Dr. Francine Kaufmann, said,

> A biographical approach reveals the sources of his interest and competency in languages, and in the three Religions of the Book, and explains how his translation of the sacred texts became...a mission of peace, and an invitation to coexistence.[83]

In the latter part of his life, Chouraqui wrote three separate autobiographies, which, although they often cover similar material, do so in very different ways, with differing emphases:

- *Ce que je crois* (Paris: B. Grasset, 1979), which was translated into English by Kenton Kilmer as *A Man in Three Worlds* (Lanham, MD: University Press of America, 1984)
- *L'amour fort comme la mort: Une autobiographie* (Love as strong as death: An autobiography) (Paris: Robert Laffont, 1990)
- *Mon testament: Le feu de l'Alliance* (My testament: The fire of the covenant) (Paris: Bayard, 2001)

A man of three worlds

Biographical details are also central to the several previous published studies of Chouraqui's work and were included in the significant obituaries published at the time of his death in July 2007. Together with the extremely thorough personal chronology that Chouraqui himself provided on his own website, these sources allow us to reconstruct his life with a fair degree of confidence and detail.

For a fully nuanced understanding of Chouraqui's passion for interreligious dialogue—which found such a unique expression in his biblical translation and commentary—we need to appreciate his upbringing and the experiences of his young adulthood before, during, and after the Second World War. As an older Chouraqui reflected back on the impact of his background on his interfaith and literary work, he wrote,

> Doubtless, it is from the multiple inheritances linked to my birth, and from the experiences of my youth, that I have drawn the strength of my desire to revive, in the unity of one source, what human beings had torn into pieces....My hope...was rooted in the search for my own identity....My translation of, and my commentaries on, the Hebrew Bible, the New Testament and the Qur'an... mark the end-point of years of delving into my own identity, and into the identity of people that I saw arguing with each in never-ending theological disputes.[84]

The Western Algerian town of Aïn-Témouchent (Arabic for "the spring of the jackal") had approximately ten thousand inhabitants in 1917, when Natân André Chouraqui was born there, the son of Isaac Chouraqui and Meléha Meyer. In his published autobiographies, Chouraqui highlights what he sees as the appropriateness of the names given to him by his parents. The three names—drawn, respectively, from Hebrew (*Natân*, from the Hebrew verb *nātan*, "to give/he has given"), Greek (*André*, from the Greek noun *anēr/andros*, "[of] a man"), and Arabic (*Chouraqui*, from the Arabic *al-Charq*, designating someone from the East)—combine to yield, roughly, "God has given a man from the East." This conjunction of three names, from three different but historically interrelated Mediterranean cultures, would foreshadow in many ways the life André Chouraqui would go on to live, as "a man in three worlds." This moniker could be understood in terms of his nationality (in turns, Algerian, French, and Israeli); in terms of his daily language (Arabic, then French, then Hebrew); and in terms of his interreligious involvements (working closely with members of the Jewish, Islamic, and Christian faiths).

The Jewish community in Algeria was a relatively small minority (less than 2 percent), within a nation that was, by the early 1900s, predominantly either French Catholic or Muslim. The family of André Chouraqui were not, however, newcomers to that land. As Sephardic Jews, they (and most of the other Jews of North Africa) boasted of a long and illustrious history in the region, dating back to the persecution of Spain's Jewish population in the fourteenth and fifteenth centuries. The Chouraquis were believed to have left Spain in 1392, a full century before the definitive expulsion of the Jews in 1492, under King Ferdinand and Queen Isabella. As Chouraqui himself would write in *Between East and West: A History of the Jews of North Africa*,

> During most periods of history, the Jews of North Africa were happier than those in most parts of Europe, where they were the objects of unrelenting hate; such extreme sentiments did not exist in the Maghreb [North African nations]. The scorn that the adherents of the different faiths expressed for each other could not obliterate the strong bonds of a common source of inspiration and a way of life intimately shared.

From the 1400s onward, the Chouraqui name can be found in historical documents from North Africa, associated with learning and scholarship. The young André grew up in a faith-filled home, steeped in the stories of his distinguished ancestors…a legacy that he was expected to live up to.

Chouraqui's father, Isaac, was a well-known grain merchant, a vintner, and community leader. For several decades, he served as president of the local Jewish congregation; he had presided over the construction of their synagogue and was a man renowned for his religious piety. It was Isaac Chouraqui who first initiated the young André into the ritual life of Judaism, and, as a devout student of the Bible and the Talmud himself, began to open up for his son some of the richness of the Hebrew, Aramaic, and Ladino languages. Even as a child, André was fascinated by the nuances of language, and by the disparity he regularly noted between the Hebrew text in his *siddur* and the less-than-satisfactory French translation that accompanied it:

> What I was reading in French rarely seemed to correspond to the Hebrew it was claiming to translate. As a child, I wondered: "Is it really that difficult to translate?" As we shall see, an entire lifetime would not be enough for me to find an answer to that question.[85]

As a boy, André grew up in a family circle where traditional religious faith was paramount ("life in our home was about praying, and praying in Hebrew") and in which the Bible held a particularly privileged place. In gratitude for the safe return of his sons and sons-in-law from the Great War, his maternal grandfather, Abraham ("Baba") Meyer, had personally commissioned the writing of a new Torah scroll for the Aïn-Témouchent synagogue. In keeping with tradition, the last few hundred letters were sketched in by the scribe but were left to be completed by members of the congregation, for whom it was a tremendous honor to fulfill this *mitzvah* (commandment). As the youngest of Meyer's grandchildren, André was given the honor of writing the final letters of Deuteronomy: "At the age of 6, I concentrated on writing the Hebrew letters properly. That was the first Bible that I made a real contribution to drafting."[86]

Aïn-Témouchent was, for all its cultural complexity, a community that was also largely ghettoized by language and religion. The French colonial sector looked down on the local Arab-speaking population (colloquially called "the Muslims," although Chouraqui says many were actually Berbers who practiced their own traditional tribal religions). The town's Catholic citizens, raised with the anti-Jewish

Une Vie Très Pleine

prejudices and stereotypes that were so deeply ingrained in Christianity at the time, viewed the local Jews with a combination of curiosity and disdain. Their treatment led to a sense of alienation and cognitive dissonance that Chouraqui described in *A Man in Three Worlds*: "The exterior world was to me a wound. My Jewish origin told me plainly, in the brutally anti-Semitic atmosphere of colonial Algeria, that I was from *elsewhere*."[87] This, in his place of birth, where his family's roots stretched back centuries. More than once, young André was the victim of anti-Jewish and anti-Semitic slurs and beatings at the hands of his schoolmates.

In André's youth, anti-Jewish riots broke out in various parts of Algeria, and Aïn-Témouchent's tiny Jewish community feared that such anti-Jewish sentiments could quickly spread to their town. André's grandfather, Baba Meyer, took matters into his own hands in a highly unusual (but ultimately successful) way: having explained the threatening situation to his employees, he organized and led them in a mini-parade down the town's main street, shouting out frighteningly accurate parodies of the racist slogans being employed in other towns. The gentle self-mockery of Meyer and company won over their neighbors, and effectively silenced any local racist partisans who were eager to make trouble. Chouraqui comments, not without a sad irony, "Even when Hitler triumphed in Europe, the anti-Semitism of our Christian neighbors never exceeded the bounds of what might be called 'good manners.'"[88]

Despite the underlying religious tensions, and the corresponding need to assert one's own religious identity, Chouraqui recalls his parents as having been quite liberal in their outlook toward both Christians and Muslims. Indeed, it was they who first taught him to appreciate the values and richness of the surrounding culture:

> If you were a "native," it was possible to be born, to live, and to die in French Algeria while hardly knowing a word of French. We lived cheek by jowl with each other, without really knowing anything about each other—and not wanting to hear anything about the others. We were segregated,

separated by a level of ignorance as inescapable as if we had been living on different planets....My father was the first person to help me to understand the beauty and the richness of another part of humanity, and another culture—that of the Muslims—about which I had never heard a single good word spoken by my French teachers....Arabic was the language of my grandparents and parents—as it had been for my ancestors for centuries. We were perfectly woven into the Muslim environment, of which we, as the Children of Israel, were an integral part—although subject, according to their laws, to a distinctive status, that of *dhimmis* or "protected ones"—from which the French presence had liberated us, by making us full-fledged citizens.[89]

André's parents, eager that he should have the best available education, did not hesitate to send him to a local Catholic kindergarten run by Salesian nuns. Although the Sisters sought to inculcate a sense of French national identity in their young charges, Chouraqui remembers his own teacher as being scrupulously respectful of the consciences of her non-Christian students:

In Sister Ubaldine's kindergarten class, and later in the primary school on Rue Pasteur, everything conspired to make me into a perfect little Frenchman, proud of his Gallic origins and culture....We were a motley crew, whom our teachers' brilliance aimed to awaken to the redeeming values of the Republic's secularity. But Sister Ubaldine would never have dreamed of trying to convince her Jewish students of the truth of Christianity. Whenever the young Christians were celebrating their rituals, or receiving catechism lessons, we were taken aside and guided in reflecting on our own religious identity.[90]

Une Vie Très Pleine

EDUCATION BOTH RELIGIOUS AND SECULAR

Such religious respect was, however, probably the *exception* in that period, rather than the *rule*. In June of 1924, seven-year-old André was physically attacked and chased by a mob of local elementary school children, who yelled anti-Jewish slurs at him as they pursued him through the streets. Safe in his home, he collapsed, trembling and feverish; the initial diagnosis was merely a cold, exacerbated by the terror of that harrowing episode. But the acute pain in his limbs soon made it clear that something other than a cold was involved; a second doctor correctly diagnosed André as suffering from an attack of childhood polio, which would leave his left leg and right arm partially paralyzed. His parents sought out the best doctors and physiotherapists available, having recourse even to renowned faith-healers and traditional cures. These various treatments, although limited in their success, at least allowed him to walk again; he would, however, have a limp for the rest of his life.

As the son of a prominent middle-class Jewish leader, André's religious education was well provided for, including private tutoring in Hebrew, in preparation for the day when he would become bar mitzvah (a son of the commandments). His curiosity about other faiths continued to grow, however, encouraged by his parents, who had many Muslim employees. As physically segregated as life in Aïn-Témouchent was, his family inculcated in him very early on an openness to, and respect for, Christianity and Islam that would guide the rest of his life.

But the deeply religious world in which he had grown up would be profoundly shaken by the experience of secondary school in Oran (a large coastal city where André went to boarding school), where his identity as a North African Jew of Spanish heritage was gradually but effectively eroded by the strictly secular French school system. Between the ages of eleven and eighteen, he was re-formed in an atheistic mold, taught to view himself as a proud descendant of classical Roman civilization, and as the intellectual heir of French rationalism.

A man of three worlds

His bar mitzvah, celebrated in the main synagogue of Aïn-Témouchent in the summer of 1929, marked his last formal link to Jewish traditions. He continued to fast on Yom Kippur (the Jewish Day of Atonement), and not to eat leavened bread during Pesach (Passover). As for everything else, however, he had become a perfect little Frenchman. He retained a few connections to the Middle East through the Arabic language and grammar classes that were offered at the Oran high school. But Western literature was his newfound passion, and during summer vacations, he read whatever he could get his hands on, especially novelists and poets (with a soft spot for the Romantics). As for God…well, he was shunted into a dusty storeroom of childhood memories.

> That was the end of my mother's stories about the miracles and wonders of our family…our ancestors…our people. That was the end of the long hours of prayer, between my father's knees in the synagogue, and during the ecstatic night-long vigils, where the chanting of the Psalms lifted us out of our weariness, our darkness and our fears, to draw us into the unspeakable light of the almighty *Elohim* [God] who was also our Father. Hebrew language and culture were forgotten about. We believed ourselves to be the Children of Israel—yes, the Hebrews, survivors of a people that thousands of years of persecutions and exile had not been able to get rid of; in the poverty of the places where we found shelter, beneath the spitting and the taunting, we remained the authentic bearers of the Bible, and almost the only ones who knew it by heart in its original language…The grace of the Republic sought to make us—Jews, Arabs or Spaniards—into true Frenchmen. From our first history class in the local school, we sang out at the top of our lungs…: "Our ancestors, the Gauls, were mighty, brave, strong and quarrelsome. Their priests were called the Druids."[91]

Une Vie Très Pleine

By the end of his secondary school years at the boarding school in Oran, André's transformation was complete:

> I was ready for Abderahmân, Donnat and Mahdad[92] to join my poor rabbis in a generalized forgetting of all the religious and Semitic things from which the Republic in its generosity had rescued me, allowing me to blossom in the bright sun of revolutionary ideas....[I decided]...not to think about the world of the Bible anymore, to forget about the Psalms and Isaiah, to abandon all religious practices, except for not eating leavened bread during Passover, and fasting devoutly on Yom Kippur. Yes, I had imperceptibly substituted one chosen people for another, shifting from my original Eastern world to this Western world, of which France seemed to be the guiding light and the hope.[93]
>
> ...I was not far from Toynbee's opinion that the Jew was an archaeological survival, a fossil. As for me, I had become, thanks to the secular and republican culture, a son of the French Revolution, a free citizen of a country whose motto—which had become mine also—was Liberty, Equality, and Fraternity.[94]
>
> We ought to have been proud of having been so generously adopted by our motherland, which rescued us from the barbarity of our past (whether that was Arab, Jewish, or sometimes even Catholic). We knew our country by heart: its hexagon was unquestionably the centre of the world, and its enlightenment....And so it was that, insidiously and almost without realizing it, I changed from one chosen people to another: *Gesta Dei per Francos!* [The deeds of God, by means of the Franks!].[95]...My cherished Bible got relegated to the storeroom of useless accessories. From kindergarten right through my doctorate from the State, having ascended through all the levels of France's educational system, I don't believe I ever heard the Bible quoted more than

A man of three worlds

two or three times, and even then, it was in passing, in a discussion of Galileo or Voltaire.[96]

In 1934, the young André completed his secondary school education. However, his leg had never fully recovered from his earlier bout of polio, and so his family arranged for him to be treated at France's La Montagne clinic, then known for its cutting-edge techniques in orthopedic surgery. The surgery was an unqualified success, but his convalescence would prove fateful for other reasons as well. The clinic was at the heart of a Protestant missionary enterprise, and André was profoundly moved to encounter young Protestant nurses who had given up comfortable lives in order to care for the sick, or to go overseas and spread the message of Christianity. He was also inspired by their obvious love for, and familiarity with, the Bible: "When I asked them questions, in order to understand the why and how of their vocation, they replied with quotations from the New Testament (about which I knew nothing) and from the Hebrew Bible, which they seemed to know better than I did."[97] They, in turn, were thrilled to discover in André a Jewish patient capable of reading and understanding the Hebrew Scriptures in their original language, and this led to many lengthy and revelatory conversations.

The experience of this profound spiritual sympathy between the Christian nurses and their Jewish patient—largely centered upon the text of the Bible—succeeded in drawing Chouraqui back to a renewed curiosity about this book that had formed such an integral part of his early life. It also convinced him that Jews and Christians had much to share with each other in terms of biblical study, a conviction that would be central to his later interfaith efforts and scholarly publications.

During one Easter vacation while still a teen, André took advantage of the break from studies to spend an extended retreat in the Saharan south of Algeria, in the oasis village of Ouargla. Here, he not only engaged in prolonged discussions about Islam with local Muslim scholars, but decided to embark on his own personal grappling with the text of the Hebrew Bible:

Une Vie Très Pleine

> I rose before daybreak. Seated in eastern fashion, like the rabbis of the oases where I lived, singing my Hebrew Psalms on the terrace of the house where I was staying, in the shadow of the palm trees....My days included from ten to twelve hours of work, struggling with the Hebrew text of the Bible, which I was trying, by translating it, to understand more deeply. At twilight...I listened to the symphony of the minarets, from which the voice of Islam sounded forth....
>
> When I headed off to Paris, where I was to pursue my studies, my atheistic convictions—which my teachers in the boarding school at Oran had tried so hard to inculcate in me—were shaken. The Bible no longer seemed to me a useless accessory, and God a waning moon. Along the way I had discovered Spinoza, to whom, for a time, I clung, as a midpoint between the atheism of my professors and that new universe, that of the God of the Bible, to whose intoxication I was soon to surrender.[98]

It was to Paris, and to the Sorbonne, that André's path led for his university studies. Philosophy was one of his greatest loves and, to compensate for his lack of classical studies in secondary school, he applied himself energetically to learning Greek and Latin on his own, in order to read the works of the great philosophers in their original languages. The writings of Baruch Spinoza (1632–77) became of particular interest (as alluded to above); here was a keen philosophical mind who seemed to combine the best of Jewish learning with a rigorous critical approach that Chouraqui found appealing, especially as regards Spinoza's (then-novel) approach to the Scriptures.

For the small-town Jewish boy from Algeria, this revelation opened the door to an entirely new way of looking at the Bible. Years of a secular education had taught him wariness of received, "institutional" interpretations, and he had drifted away from the Bible, seeing it merely as a collection of irrelevant myths and legends. But here was Spinoza, a brilliant intellectual who was bringing the tools of scientific inquiry to bear on the text and meaning of the Bible. It was a significant discovery, one that would continue to inspire Chouraqui's own vision for decades to come.

Having weighed the options, he and his family decided that he was best suited to progress to studies in law, which he began in November 1935. He was thoroughly entranced by the political, academic, and social life of Paris—but, as he admits, the sinister shadows of growing anti-Semitism were already beginning to appear, presaging the sufferings and horrors to come. Distinctions of religion were almost meaningless in the midst of such a diverse (and largely secular) student body, although some of André's friends were intrigued by his Jewish heritage and did not hesitate to ask him questions about Judaism. "We felt ourselves at home in Paris, at the University, among our teachers or with our fellow students. Gone, or almost gone, was the obsessive fear of being rejected on account of being Jewish."[99]

Those years of study at the Sorbonne would prove to be the most spiritually transformative of his young adult life. Chouraqui points to February 10, 1937, as a particular *kairos* moment: he experienced what he describes as an "illumination"—a moment of mystical insight that radically convinced him, once and for all, of the reality and presence of God in the universe, and in his own life. This experience of the Ineffable completely reoriented him. Now he became increasingly absorbed in studying the Bible and its commentaries, and in struggling with the subtleties and complex riches of biblical translation. The Bible literally became his companion, and its words and ideas permeated almost every waking moment.

Immersed in a predominantly Catholic Christian culture, Chouraqui found a new stimulus in the way in which the stories and images of the Bible had taken shape in the art and architecture of the great cathedrals, and in so much of the musical heritage of Europe.

> It was in Paris that I discovered Christian art, and Christianity....In Paris, sitting in front of the façade of Notre-Dame and lost in admiration, I contemplated the kings of Israel who seemed, with Jesus and his mother, to be

Une Vie Très Pleine

watching over the life of the capital....I discovered the many faces of a type of art that was entirely born out of the Bible's fertile soil.

CHOURAQUI'S REDISCOVERY OF JUDAISM

Despite his obvious appreciation for much of Christianity, however, Chouraqui had no intention of abandoning the faith of his ancestry. In fact, his years in prewar France did much to kindle in him a consciousness of—and a passionate recommitment to—his Jewish identity. This reawakening was in part a reaction to his contact with Christians, whose faith challenged him to think more seriously about his own, and in part by his discovery of a stream of Jewish thinking that explored the Bible outside traditional interpretations and categories. But it was also sparked by the steadily rising tide of anti-Jewish rhetoric, public demonstrations, and violence, which Chouraqui already sensed were the harbingers of much darker times for Europe's Jews. If he were to suffer—and perhaps die—on account of his Jewishness, he wished to deliberately unite himself to the faith for which he might one day perish:

> It took...the shock of my discovery of God, through my encounter with Christian and Muslim spirituality, and the trauma of the Hitlerian persecution, to pull me back to my Jewish well-springs. Since Hitler wanted to take my life because I was Jewish, at least I wanted to die with my eyes open, knowing what it meant to be Jewish.[100]

André's *teshuvah*, or spiritual rediscovery, led him to take further concrete steps. In late April of 1937, he wrote to the director of France's rabbinical seminary, asking to be admitted to its course of studies. Although he did not wish to become a rabbi, he was in search of teachers who could help him to embark on a systematic, in-depth study of the Hebrew Bible and Jewish religious literature. The seminary's head, Chief Rabbi Maurice Liber, welcomed André's passionate interest, although with some perplexity: why would a brilliant young law student (he was not quite twenty) seek rabbinic studies, if he had no intention of becoming either a rabbi or a cantor?

André's obvious zeal, his scholastic aptitude—and the fact of his family's reputation, known even in French circles—gained him admission and he began remedial Hebrew classes. In October, his rabbinic studies, properly speaking, began. Side by side with his legal courses, André engaged in the study of Scripture and Talmud, renewing and furthering his familiarity with the Hebrew of his childhood, and gradually gaining fluency in Aramaic as well.

Although he found the seminary itself somewhat down-at-the-heel, and some of its courses unoriginal or overly orthodox for his tastes, nevertheless the years of his rabbinic education left Chouraqui with a deep admiration for the wealth of Jewish erudition that never left him. They also enabled him to study under some unquestioned masters, whose creativity and penetrating thought rewarded his efforts. In a poignant admission, Chouraqui writes in retrospect that, had he and his fellow students been able to guess at the fate that awaited many of these same professors, they would, almost certainly, have taken those studies—and their own friendships as students—more seriously:

> If we had known then that the majority of our teachers and fellow-students at the school would, only three years later, be deported and exterminated in the camps of Nazi Germany, our outlook on reality—and the way we dealt with each other—would have been so very different.... The faces of so many of my friends, who lost their freedom, and their lives...still haunt my memory....Our happy gang had absolutely no idea of the fate that awaited us.[101]

André's rabbinic studies were no impediment to his ongoing legal studies at university and, in June 1938, he graduated with his law degree. Although he seemed eminently suited for graduate studies, events elsewhere in Europe cast their shadow over his life, both as a student and as a recommitted Jew.

Une Vie Très Pleine

THE RAVAGES OF WAR

By Chouraqui's account, none of the faculty at the rabbinic college seriously considered that Hitler's rise to power was anything other than a blip on the radar screen of German political history, soon to be corrected, with no direct consequences for their own lives or mission. Even the signal devastation of *Kristallnacht*, and the growing territorial aggression of Nazi Germany under Hitler, did not shake the conviction of Chouraqui's French contemporaries that they personally had nothing to fear from the Nazi threat. Chouraqui himself was vacationing with his family in Algeria as the tensions mounted in Europe; recuperating from a serious bicycle accident, he followed with trepidation the unfolding drama in Europe, which threatened to overturn the comfortable university student life to which he had become accustomed. He had just returned to France to continue his studies at the rabbinic seminary when, on September 3, 1939, France and Britain formally declared war on Germany.

The first months of the war were a time of great anxiety, uncertainty, and fear. For André, however, they also marked the beginnings of a relationship that would mark his life forever. The young woman's name was Colette Boyer, and, at the insistence of a mutual friend, she and André met on November 11, 1939.[102] Colette was a gifted pianist and composer who was, however, often confined to bed with a grave form of tuberculosis. While Chouraqui was immediately struck by her beauty and intelligence, their initial conversation quickly revealed a depth of religious-mystical questing that resonated with his own; she confided in him her sense of a contemplative monastic vocation. It was not long before they had become intimate friends, their discussions always focusing on the things of God and on the Bible. Colette, nominally a Catholic, was thrilled to discover that André was Jewish and skilled in biblical study; she herself had arrived at a determination to study Hebrew on her own, in order to better understand the Bible.

Colette's personal sufferings had also given her a deep sensitivity for the sufferings of others, and she felt a particular solidarity with the Jews. What originally began as a friendship quickly progressed to what Chouraqui describes as a relationship of two soulmates. They saw themselves as spiritual brother and sister, and they soon realized that they were destined to be married. Even when separated by distance, they maintained an often-daily correspondence, and André declared that, so far as he was concerned, Colette's health condition constituted no obstacle to their union. He returned home to Algeria for the spring break of 1940 and, despite protests from family and friends (who implored him to seek safe passage to the United States), he decided to return to Paris in late May 1940; he felt compelled to stand alongside his French and Jewish friends in the battle that was ready to erupt. And he desperately wanted to be with Colette, whatever might happen.

In June of 1940, France was invaded by both the Germans and the Italians. Having remained as long as he judged prudent, André now took Colette with him on his bicycle, and they joined the interminable convoys fleeing Paris. He eventually brought Colette to the safety of her sister's home near Orléans, and he set out alone in the hope of finding some way back to Algeria. Colette came to meet him in Marseille, and their parting there was bitter and emotional, neither knowing if they would ever see each other again. Having arrived in Algeria, André waited several agonizing months for news from her, and was stunned when, on November 8, he received word that Colette was pregnant; would he agree to take responsibility for both mother and child? He sent her the money for the boat trip to Algeria, all the time wondering how he would support them.

Colette and André sought to marry in a Jewish religious ceremony, but the local Algerian rabbi attempted to discourage them: if Colette were to convert to Judaism, it would obviously place both mother and child in harm's way. Colette was insistent: although formally baptized a Catholic, she had never truly considered herself a Christian, and her intensive studies of Hebrew and of Judaism with André had convinced her that her path to God lay in embracing the Jewish faith. Rabbi Rouche finally conceded, agreeing to lead Colette through an accelerated course preparing her for conversion. When she stood before the board of three rabbis who were to examine her on her knowledge of Judaism, "having questioned her, they stated that she knew Judaism at least as well, if not better, than most of our own mothers and sisters."[103] Her conversion ceremony took place on December 10, 1940. On December 23, Colette and André were married in a traditional Jewish ceremony (the circumstances dictated that the usual civil marriage was inadvisable, since such a public act could only further compromise Colette's safety).

In the meantime, the collaborationist Vichy government had been proceeding with the implementation of the Nazis' anti-Semitic directives. France's Jews became subject to increasingly strict limitations and, in Algeria, the Crémieux decree of 1870 (conferring French citizenship on its Jewish citizens) was revoked; Jews were no longer considered French citizens and could no longer hold broad categories of jobs in political, social, and economic life. Chouraqui, realizing that his legal career was now untenable, resigned his position as a barrister on June 14, 1941.

Because of Colette's delicate medical condition, their doctor admitted her to hospital in advance of the expected delivery date. Their daughter was named Emmanuèle, but her health was precarious from birth, and the baby lived only three months. Colette left for a French sanatorium to recover, and André himself returned to France at the end of October 1941, eventually setting out for Clermont-Ferrand, the rabbinical school's new home. Deprivation and hardship were the order of the day and André, anguished after the events of the previous months, threw himself into his studies with a mixture of despair and obsession: "My shock at being uprooted was softened once I got back to my studies—Bible, Talmud, Jewish and Christian theologies."[104] André's studies were, however, overshadowed, first by the medically necessary abortion of Colette's second child in July 1942—but also by his growing awareness of the atrocities being committed elsewhere against the Jews by the Nazis. He describes the terror and the response: "More and more detailed—and more and more horrific—reports were reaching me from the concentration camps in France and Germany. We were trying to find cribs for the hundreds of babies born to Jewish women who had been assaulted by their persecutors, and safe shelters for the thousands of people who had been reduced to despair."[105]

ENDURING THE WAR AND ITS REPERCUSSIONS

As 1942 progressed, the situation for France's Jews grew more dire with each passing week. The German army made repeated incursions into Clermont-Ferrand, arresting hundreds of university professors and students, including many of André's classmates and friends. In late June, new government regulations confiscated Jewish properties and began the process of arresting and deporting local Jews; during the early summer, Jews were formally expelled from the region of Clermont-Ferrand. The rabbinical college was disbanded as its students fled or were arrested. In desperation, Chouraqui wrote to the chief rabbi in Paris, begging him to protest publicly against these anti-Jewish measures. The "Final Solution" had been decreed and was rapidly being implemented in occupied Europe.

Eventually, André succeeded in finding a safe refuge for Colette: a doctor friend offered them the use of his family farm in Chaumergeais, both as a home and as a nerve center for the covert work André had begun, trying to arrange provisions, safe houses, and passage for Jews and others in flight. In quiet collaboration with the residents and several local churches, he helped to set up a remarkable supply network that provided food, medicine, and baby supplies to mothers, young children, and the elderly in safe houses. Several local Christian pastors encouraged their parishioners to take in persecuted Jews, especially threatened children, and even used their Sunday liturgies to solicit—subtly but effectively—the needed shelter and supplies:

> Pastors Leenhardt, Trocmé, Theiss and others encouraged their flocks to welcome persecuted Jews. When I didn't have any places for my children, the Sunday sermon in the Protestant churches would invariably focus on the theme of "Whatsoever you do to the least of these children, you do it to Me." Hearts and doors were opened to

such a degree that, right up until the Liberation, not a single one of my children, and not a single one of my refugees, was lost. When they arrived at one of the stations where the train stopped, the villagers were there—two, three or four of them—eager to see the faces of their adoptive children. Their smiles told me that these children would not be lacking for anything.[106]

Chouraqui became a member of the French Resistance cells active in the Haute-Loire region, passing messages in code and serving as a conduit for the transport of people, food, medicine, and other supplies.[107] He also managed to regularly gather groups of Jewish colleagues and friends, who formed underground study circles (which they called "the School of the Prophets") led by Jewish intellectuals in hiding. Chouraqui refused to allow the atrocities of war to entirely sideline his academic ambitions or undermine his renewed sense of his Jewish self; his subversive activities began to take on both a material and an intellectual quality.

During this period, Chouraqui also renewed an old friendship with the Algerian-born absurdist philosopher (and fellow Resistance fighter) Albert Camus, and the two engaged in discussions about God, morality, and the Bible. In *Albert Camus: A Biography*, Herbert Lottman suggests the relationship must have been of comfort to both men: "Outsider that he was, Camus didn't know these good people and they had little opportunity to get to know him. He did meet one old friend from Algeria here, André Chouraqui....Camus visited Chouraqui regularly and they would dine on couscous, talk about Camus' work; it helped relieve Camus' anxiety to be with someone from his own country."[108]

Literary historian Patrick Henry notes, "An important biblical scholar who would later translate the Hebrew Bible into French, Chouraqui helped Camus decipher the significance of the plague in the Bible as he worked on *La Peste* in Panelier, and invited him to his hideout in Chaumargeais, a hamlet in the village of Tence, where they would talk at length about their situation and eat Algerian cuisine."[109]

A man of three worlds

Adds Henry, in *We Only Know Men: The Rescue of Jews in France during the Holocaust*:

> It is abundantly clear, as Camus himself states against certain critics of this work, that among other things, *The Plague* portrays allegorically the European struggle against Nazism.[110]

Chouraqui, who refers to Camus as "the anti-prophet of our time," says they would often meet one another at night, and engage in long philosophical conversations over "the food of our native Algeria, whose taste he was almost forgetting":

> [Camus] asked me to read him the passages of the Scriptures which dealt with the plague. "'Plague' occurs 49 times in the Bible. In Hebrew, the word is *dèbèr*, which is very close to *dabar*, the Word, the term that the Greeks would translate as *logos*." "So a plague, then, would be the consequence of the Word being deformed?" he asked. "… In our kabbalists, there are lots of teachings that would lean in that direction: betray the *dabar* and you have *dèbèr*; kill the Word and you have plagues: blood, famine and war." "And here we are, right in the middle of it, caught like rats, caught in the trap of our own madness," [Camus] concluded.[111]

Chouraqui tells this story in *L'amour fort comme la mort*. He argues that Camus was actually profoundly religious, but that his view of God was so exacting and pure that it could not find a home in any human religious system: "He was too demanding to be satisfied with the God that any of the religions and their spokespersons described."

Chouraqui's wartime experiences offered him powerful new insights into religion, and into the possibilities for interreligious cooperation. While he was scandalized and disappointed by the failure of many religious Christians to offer moral or practical assistance to their persecuted brethren, nevertheless he encountered many followers of

Christ who were generous and courageous in their efforts, and who saw their work as simply the lived expression of their Christian calling. Similarly, he was amazed to see how, in the ranks of the Resistance, religious categories largely fell away or became irrelevant, subsumed in a larger, shared mission. Jews, Catholics, and Protestants did not hesitate to fight and die side by side with communists and avowed atheists. Surely, Chouraqui thought, such spiritual and ethical camaraderie—which was evidently possible—need not be limited to the most harrowing moments of humanity?

> [In the ranks of the Resistance] the pariahs that we had become recognized one another, not by their religion, but by the intensity of their suffering, the courage of their fighting, and the boldness of their hope. Among us we counted Jews, Christians, Moslems, and freethinkers, ready to offer their lives that freedom might be won and that life might triumph over death....*As night ended and dawn blazed forth, I would be seized again by the same vision of the return, of the liberation, of universal brotherhood, of peace.*[112]

Colette and André returned to Paris in October 1944, after the city's liberation, but those postliberation months left him confused and depressed, as he grappled with the implications of these questions. Surely such intuitions could form the basis of a new and more fraternal Europe...but were there men and women willing to embrace these ideas in practice? What he and others had undergone during the war left him somewhat skeptical:

> Even France, the well-beloved France of my studies and of my nightly watching, she to whom I owed my language and my culture, had consented that I should be cast out from her bosom, and that I be reduced to the condition of a pariah. On the parvis in front of Notre Dame, I contemplated the statue representing the Synagogue, blindfolded, and holding a broken sceptre, by the side of her triumphant sister, the

Church....Thirty-three centuries of Mosaic religion, two thousand years of Christianity, came to their climax in the bankruptcy of the Second World War.[113]

RETURN TO ALGERIA—AND THE START OF A GLOBAL CAREER

As soon as he could, André returned to his native Algeria, where he was named a regional justice of the peace. He continued his legal studies at the University of Algiers, earning in 1946 a further specialization in Algerian, Tunisian, and Moroccan law. In the summer of 1947, Chouraqui made a friendship that would have a decisive influence on his life and career. He met René Cassin, a distinguished French jurist and humanitarian who was the president of the Alliance Israélite Universelle (AIU), one of Europe's major Jewish organizations. Cassin, impressed by Chouraqui, hired him on in November of that year as deputy general secretary of the AIU; Chouraqui also took on new national responsibilities, working to rebuild postwar Jewish life in France and across a ravaged Europe.

Chouraqui's work with the AIU took him literally around the world, nurturing a broad network of contacts with Jewish communities in every corner of the globe. Working together with UNICEF's NGO branch, he inspected educational and other cultural and humanitarian works supported by Jewish organizations, and worked as a spokesperson and liaison for Europe's Jewish communities on the world stage. He was also a public speaker very much in demand, giving conferences and speaking at public events throughout the world.

A landmark moment in the history of modern Jewish-Christian relations occurred in 1948, with the foundation in Paris of the first Amitié judéo-chrétienne (Jewish–Christian Friendship Association), chapters of which would later be established in Aix-en-Provence, Marseille, Montpellier, Nîmes, Lyon, and Lille. Its founders included the French Jewish historian Jules Isaac (sometimes called the "godfather" of modern Jewish–Christian dialogue), Edmond Fleg, and Henri Marrou, and its circle would at various times include Jacob Kaplan (the chief rabbi of France), as well as Catholic priests Michel

Une Vie Très Pleine

Riquet and Paul Démann, and the priest-theologian (and later cardinal) Jean Daniélou. From a very early stage, Chouraqui was closely involved with this fledgling movement (one French article calls him one of its "instigators"), and he was a close friend of its leaders. He and Jules Isaac had met and become friends years earlier, in a very different setting:

> On a day in November 1942, someone told me, "Go to near Saint-Agrève, a man has need for false identity and ration cards so he can continue to live a clandestine existence, his name is Jules Isaac." I went immediately and there, before my eyes, to my astonishment (having graduated from university), was none other than the author of the books that had been a part of my secondary curriculum. We shook hands. He seated himself at a table from which he picked up a thin notebook, which he handed me when he learned that I was a student at the *École Rabbinique de France*, that I had an interest in the Bible and that I could read Hebrew. I can see in my mind's eye this thin notebook whose pages were covered by Jules Isaac's script, so beautiful, so clear, so firm, so honest and so solid. He had penned a title on the cover page of this thin notebook: "Christians, do not forget!"[114]
>
> After the war, I encountered Jules Isaac again—by the greatest stroke of coincidence—on the very first day I returned to Paris after its liberation I was having lunch in a restaurant on the Rue des Écoles, when all of a sudden my gaze was drawn to a face that was not unfamiliar to me, which I sought to make out under the beard that adorned it. The person who had just come in sat down at a table next to mine, and began to talk. No longer was there any possible doubt…it was the voice of Jules Isaac. We stood up together and we embraced silently. He explained that he had not immediately recognized me because I was now beardless.… When we had last seen each other, at a boarding-house near Chambon-sur-Lignon, Jules Isaac had been the clean-shaven

one, while mine was the face adorned with the bushy beard of a Resistance fighter. At that time (it was in 1942), I had had the privilege of giving him forged food ration and identity cards, which allowed him to get by during the harshest period of the occupation. But most of all, I had had the privilege of discussing with him about the problem that so much concerned me: the problem of Christian anti-Semitism. I can still see the little student notebook that he showed me during our first meeting, on the cover of which he had written, in his careful handwriting: "Christians, do not forget!" His wife, his daughter and his son-in-law were still alive at the time. It was only later that that notebook would become the voluminous and incomparable *Jesus and Israel*, which opens with a heart-wrenching and unforgettable dedication: "To my wife and my daughter—martyrs—killed by the Germans, killed simply because their name was 'Isaac.'"[115]

We know from their surviving correspondence that Isaac and Chouraqui had already been in discussions about the most appropriate approach to these issues. In a letter of September 10, 1945 (just a year after the liberation of France, and only four months after the end of the war), Chouraqui wrote to Isaac,

> Is not what unites us to the Christians more important than what separates us from them? And has not the time for a Judeo-Christian *rapprochement*, for a reunion, arrived, in this time when we have in common our millions of martyrs?…Jesus and Israel seem to me infinitely closer than Jews (and Christians too, usually) believe.[116]

Like Jules Isaac, Chouraqui's bitter wartime experiences left him with profound questions about the roots of the Christian hatred of the Jews—and committed to overturning it. He clearly believed that, in the wake of the horrors of the war, the only viable path forward lay in a concrete dialogue between Jews and Christians, in breaking down the walls of misunderstanding, ignorance, and prejudice that had traditionally kept the two faiths at arm's length. Already in the immediate aftermath of the war, Chouraqui was active in the beginnings of Jewish-Christian relations in France. As he later acknowledged (in a 1963 tribute to Jules Isaac), however, those beginnings were met with a great deal of cynicism and suspicion at the time:

> When the *Amitiés judéo-chrétiennes* [Jewish–Christian Friendship Associations] were just getting started—just 15 years ago!—they provoked skeptical or ironic smirks from people here and there. The wise men of the world shrugged their shoulders, wondering where all of this could lead. Some people believed that, instead of friendship, this was actually a strategic calculation—on the part of the Jews, calculated to allow them to escape from the nasty consequences of anti-Semitism…and also on the part of the Christians, who were eager to find an "in" with the Jews, in order to convert them. And maybe for some people, that was all the *Amitiés judéo-chrétiennes* were… but that was not the reality.[117]

Chouraqui's firsthand experience of the energy and idealism of such postwar interreligious initiatives further reinforced his own sense of the necessity of formal structures for interfaith dialogue and collaboration. He would go on to found, and to actively support, a number of similar organizations on the local, national, and international levels. In the summer of 1948, Chouraqui's mentor Jules Isaac was a leading figure in the now-famous gathering of Catholics, Protestants, and Jews called the Seelisberg Conference, whose pioneering document, the Ten Points of Seelisberg, called for a dramatic revision of Christian attitudes toward Jews. A few months later, on November 15, 1948, Chouraqui defended his groundbreaking doctoral thesis at the Sorbonne, on the legal aspects of the creation of the new state of Israel—quite likely the first thesis dedicated to the legal aspects of the birth of the reborn Jewish state. Chouraqui found himself intimately bound up with the beginnings of Jewish-Christian dialogue, and the establishment of the State of

THE ADVENT OF *NOSTRA AETATE*

Chouraqui's friendship with Jules Isaac would also link him, though indirectly, with one of the other major turning points of modern Jewish-Christian history: the deliberations of the Second Vatican Council (1962–65). Isaac's books—*Jésus et Israël* (Jesus and Israel, 1948), *Genèse de l'antisémitisme* (The genesis of antisemitism, 1956), and *L'enseignement du mépris* (The teaching of contempt, 1962)—had distilled down years of careful historical and theological analysis of longstanding Christian claims about Jews.

Isaac had, however, failed to secure any reforms in Catholicism as a result of a 1949 meeting with Pope Pius XII. With the 1958 election of Cardinal Angelo Roncalli as Pope John XXIII, Isaac saw the potential for possible dialogue with a former Vatican diplomat who had distinguished himself in his wartime efforts to protect and save threatened Jews. When, in January 1959, Pope John announced the convoking of an ecumenical council of all the world's Catholic bishops to modernize Catholic life, Isaac's hopes were lifted. On June 13, 1960, he had an audience with the pope, during which he presented a synthesis of his findings. The octogenarian historian asked the octogenarian pope that the upcoming Council take a firm stand against anti-Semitism, and reform traditional anti-Jewish teachings and prayers in Catholic life.

"May I leave with some hope?" Isaac asked as he departed. "You have a right to more than just hope," the Pope famously replied. Isaac's research, subsequently placed into the hands of Cardinal Augustin Bea and a team of Catholic theological experts, would provide the foundations for one of the Council's most hotly argued and eagerly awaited documents. The original 1962 schema of a "Decree on the Jews" became, via a tortuous and intrigue-riddled path, a conciliar "declaration on the Church's relationship to non-Christian religions," promulgated on October 28, 1965. Entitled *Nostra aetate* ("In our time"), its tightly worded paragraph 4 on Judaism was the source of much celebration and some consternation. It was not everything its advocates had hoped for, but it was much more than what some of the more conservative bishops were entirely comfortable with. For the first time, the Catholic Church had issued a formal teaching document confirming the validity of the Jewish covenant, denouncing anti-Semitism and racism, and rejecting the assignment of responsibility for Christ's death to the Jewish people as a whole. Limited though it might be, it was—as the media and Jewish commentators agreed—a revolutionary step forward in Jewish-Christian rapprochement.

ANDRÉ AND COLETTE: A PAINFUL PARTING

Colette's health, never robust, had by this time become increasingly precarious, and she retired to the village of St-Maximin for rest and medical care. In her physical weakness, she turned more and more to a contemplative life of prayer and biblical study, often caught up in ecstatic experiences of intimacy with God. She urged André to move with her to Jerusalem, a city she had long dreamed of, but he realized that the medical facilities of the newborn state were not yet adequate to meet her increasing health needs. They discussed a separation, and Colette began to look toward the Catholic Church, in which she now believed she could live her desired way of life while continuing to maintain her sense of Hebraic identity. In August 1948, they decided to separate—not because of lack of love, but simply because the central loves in their lives were leading them in different directions. The Little Sisters of Jesus (an order of nuns inspired by the French soldier-monk Charles de Foucauld) welcomed Colette (although Jewish and married) into one of their homes. On December 25, 1948, Colette was received into the Catholic Church by the archbishop of Aix-en-Provence, as André watched—insisting, however, that she was by no means turning her back on her Jewish identity and adherence:

> Since there was not any contemplative life possible in a synagogue setting, and since I was stubbornly refusing to go and settle with her in Israel, she turned toward the Catholic Church—but without ever breaking with her Hebraic faithfulness....She wanted to withdraw to a convent, which would allow her to deepen her Hebrew studies, while also pursuing her inner quest, the incessant struggle in which she had been engaged, to grasp the depths of human nature, and to see the God she adored, face-to-face.[118]

It was a bittersweet parting for André; although he understood Colette's attraction to a contemplative life of prayer and study, nevertheless he found himself initially racked with jealousy, anger, and resentment: "I sometimes found myself thinking that my pain would have been more bearable if my wife had abandoned me for another man, and not for this God who was tearing her away from me."[119] With the passage of time, however, Colette and André's relationship began to shift. No longer spouses, they maintained a surprisingly intimate relationship, a regular correspondence, and occasional visits, until Colette's death more than thirty years later, in 1981. Chouraqui wrote of Colette, "Having ceased to be my wife in terms of our civil status, she became my sister and, in some ways, a mother to me."[120]

THE PROMISED LAND BECKONS; LITERARY BEGINNINGS

In July 1950, André traveled for the first time to Israel. From his earliest childhood, he had entertained romantic visions of the Holy Land, and especially of the holy city of Jerusalem. The reality, however, was far different. He was traumatized to see how the beauty of Jerusalem had been tarnished by the tragedies of the War of Independence, leaving many casualties on a human level and tremendous damage on the level of buildings and infrastructure. The cease-fire border divided the city in half; the holy places that had filled

André's mind for a lifetime were tantalizingly close—but frustratingly out of reach:

> Jerusalem was both present to, and absent from, Jerusalem. The dream of return had been smashed, against the concrete and barbed-wire wall that separated Jerusalem from Jerusalem. It had taken us twenty centuries to return from the four corners of the planet, only to see our momentum halted a few metres from our goal. The city's trembling heart—the Temple Mount, which constitutes its centre—rose in front of our eyes, but it was more inaccessible than if it had been located on another planet.[121]

For six years, Chouraqui would undertake several further trips to Israel, each of them rooting his mind and heart more deeply in its ancient soil, until it was only a matter of time before he realized he must make his own *aliyah*, or immigration, to the land from which his distant ancestors had been exiled almost nineteen hundred years earlier.

> Yes, discovering Jerusalem was overwhelming for me: the city offered a type of wine that I had never tasted before. For the first time, I felt at home…for the first time, I belonged to a country whose soil would never again be pulled out from under my feet.[122]

> Seeing Jerusalem hit me with the force of a revelation. It kindled within me an absolute determination: to link myself personally to the effort to build up Israel. Each of my trips anchored me more deeply in that desire.[123]

The year 1950 also saw the publication of Chouraqui's first two books: his translation (undertaken during his wartime service in the Resistance) of the eleventh-century Jewish philosopher and rabbi Baḥya ibn Paquda's *Duties of the Heart*, and a work on the legal situation of Moroccan Jews, *La Condition juridique de l'Israélite marocain*. Its publication marked the first of many books Chouraqui would write on political and politico-religious themes, marking him out as a knowledgeable, passionate, and articulate commentator on some of the most sensitive of twentieth-century topics. With his combination of legal and religious training, he sought to bring to bear on these highly explosive issues the best and most creative thinking, capable of building bridges and fostering justice and reconciliation. For Chouraqui, these were not abstract geopolitical questions, but matters that were deeply ingrained in his own individual, national, and religious histories, and in which he felt a personal stake.

The text by ibn Paquda would equally establish Chouraqui's reputation as a careful and sensitive literary translator, and his work was widely praised by French intellectuals. Chouraqui's first literary translation, the fruit of years of reflection on language and religion, was an instant success, and his potential in this field was widely acknowledged (indeed, his translation of ibn Paquda has remained in print for more than half a century, republished most recently in 2002). For those who had eyes to see, however, it was more than merely a beautiful literary production. Chouraqui's choice of a key Judeo-Arabic text from the Golden Age of Spain's Christian-Jewish-Muslim *convivencia* signaled his own vision and hope for a similar modern-day cooperation of the Abrahamic faiths. It was an impulse that increasingly captured his imagination and inspired his activity.

In November 1951, his translation of the Song of Songs was published and, in 1955, an edition of the Book of Psalms. However, his biblical translations—hailed for their fidelity and linguistic dexterity—would be overtaken by his growing literary output on other topics, and he would only return to the Bible—his first and greatest love—decades later.

ALIYAH AND A NEW POLITICAL LIFE

The year 1956 would be a decisive one, both for Chouraqui and for his life's work. From August to November—during the Suez Crisis—he lived in Israel, involved in various meetings and discussions with the Israeli government. With the support of the Israeli leadership, he established on December 29 what he called the Comité pour l'Entente religieuse en Israël et dans le monde (Committee for religious understanding in Israel and in the world), a group that would work to actively build up relationships of trust and understanding among Jews, Christians, and Muslims:

> When I went there this time, it was not on Alliance Israélite business, but to found an interreligious committee that brought together Jews, Christians and Muslims—the first of its kind in the country—based on a broadening of our Amitiés judéo-chrétiennes in France, or the Amitiés monothéistes in Algeria.[124]

Chouraqui met with Prime Minister David Ben-Gurion and was invited to present his ideas during a public lecture in the presence of Israel's president, Yitzhak Ben-Zvi. His experiences convinced him that the time had come to finally emigrate to Israel. In 1958, he married Annette Levy, a liberal Jewish activist and physiotherapist sixteen years his junior, who had first come to know him through his lectures around Paris. Later that year, the couple made their long-anticipated *aliyah*. Initially, André and Annette settled in the Rehov Hovevei Sion area of Jerusalem. However, André had his sights set on a more permanent location: a lot on Aïn-Rogel Street—only meters from the Jordanian border, a regular flashpoint of tensions and violence. It is there that they would live until André's death.

> This land that I was discovering, wonder-struck…was the land of the Bible. The Hebrew that I was beginning to learn to speak, after having read it—from my earliest youth, when I could only babble it—was the language of the Bible. I was a forty-something infant, and I was learning my paternal tongue all over again, in order to finally speak it—the language of the Book of Books, which had been my first love…I knew biblical Hebrew as a dead language, but my theoretical knowledge was an obstacle rather than a help when it came to putting it into practice.[125]

A man of three worlds

After his arrival in Jerusalem, it did not take long for Chouraqui—already well-known among Israel's governing class and cultural élite—to find himself at the heart of the country's political and religious life. A growing friendship with Ben-Gurion led to Chouraqui's nomination to a cabinet-level position, as Advisor for the Integration of Ethnic Communities (1958–64). As a North African Jew, the issue was near and dear to André's heart; indeed, he had witnessed some of the discrimination to which many of his fellow Mizrahi immigrants (Jews from Arab-speaking countries) had been subjected. He lobbied for changes to government policies, arguing for the necessity of superior-level educational opportunities for the large immigrant populace, as a foundation for Israel's growth, social cohesion, and future prosperity.

> To tell the truth, Ben-Gurion was constantly intrigued by the blend he perceived in me—a typical Maghrebin [North African Jew], Sephardic, with a government doctorate from the University of Paris—who was, nonetheless, genuinely Jewish, fresh out of the Rabbinic College of France—and a Zionist to boot!...I accepted the title of advisor to the cabinet chairman, for the integration of [ethnic] communities....The ingredients from which I was to mix my recipe were Jews who had come from 102 countries around the world, who spoke more than 80 languages, half of them representing the East and half of them representing the West of the planet. We had to prepare for the harmonious coming-together of this unprecedented multitude, trying to forge from them a new nation.[126]

It was a difficult and sometimes thankless task, with almost no resources. Even Chouraqui's push for better educational opportunities for immigrants was met with occasional skepticism from his own colleagues within the cabinet, such as Deputy Education Minister Ami Assaf, a *sabra* who was convinced that many of the immigrants suffered from a congenital intellectual inferiority that left them with little hope of educational success.

Une Vie Très Pleine

Perhaps his most intimate and lasting relationship with Ben-Gurion, however, centered around the informal "biblical circles" that the prime minister regularly held at his residence, to which Chouraqui was invited, during which the country's top biblical scholars and archaeologists were asked to share their findings and insights:

> It was on the level of the Bible that I had my most meaningful communication with Ben-Gurion. The book had shaped his thinking since his childhood, and throughout his whole life, it provided him with an inexhaustible pool of historical, theological, and sometimes even political, references, which he endeavored to apply to the concrete situations in which he had to lead his people. When he had to confront the failings of his Socialism and Zionism, the Bible was for him the ultimate point of reference; he always found answers there to his questions, not to mention the great prophetic inspiration that he needed to overcome his daily difficulties. Ben-Gurion knew the Bible as few specialists do. He lived it out, as a document of timeless relevance.[127]
>
> Focused on the Bible, Ben-Gurion learned Greek in order to read Plato in the original, and Spanish in order to better understand Cervantes....But the Bible remained his essential source of inspiration.[128]

When Haim Gevaryahu, the leader of Israel's biblical movement, suggested setting up a Bible-study group at his home, Ben-Gurion didn't hesitate for a second:
"So, when can we start, and how long should the sessions be?"
"An hour and a half," Haim prudently answered.
"An hour and a half? But that's not enough time!"

The group should meet at sundown and study the Bible until dawn, before wrapping up its study with a walk in the Judean hills, which are so stunningly beautiful in the light of the rising sun! That is where the Bible was born, and that is where it is possible to understand it best.

Our biblical group met for the first time on 4 December 1958, in the presence of the country's best biblical scholars.... We were surrounded by university professors and specialists, for whom it is no exaggeration to say that they knew the Bible almost by heart.

Whenever the Bible was being discussed, the Old Man became animated, and his face lit up. He became, once more, the young child back in Plonsk, between his grandfather's knees, who was learning to read and discuss the Bible.[129]

Chouraqui's term as advisor lasted for almost six years, ending in 1964, in the wake of Ben-Gurion's own resignation.

MUNICIPAL POLITICS IN JERUSALEM

September 30, 1965, was a particularly momentous day for Jewish-Christian relations. As mentioned earlier, the Second Vatican Council, convoked by Pope John XXIII, was set to approve *Nostra aetate*, its landmark document on Catholic attitudes toward non-Christians. Chouraqui had been personally invited by the Council's secretary-general, Bishop Pericle Felici, to attend the official conciliar vote on the declaration, as the Alliance Israélite's observer-delegate.

> Very early in the morning, I attended the Solemn Mass celebrating Jerome, who was, out of all the saints on the Catholic calendar, the one who had known the most Hebrew; it was not by chance that the document on non-Christian religions had been distributed under his patronage. Over the course of that day, in addition to meeting good Pope John XXIII, I met more cardinals, archbishops and bishops than had all of my ancestors together since the creation of the world.[130]

Returning to his hotel after the day's events, André was surprised to discover a series of urgent messages waiting for him, from his friend and political colleague Teddy Kollek in Jerusalem. Kollek was running in the upcoming municipal elections, as a candidate for mayor of Jerusalem; would Chouraqui agree to run as his deputy? Chouraqui was by now a well-known and respected figure among Jerusalem's immigrant groups, for whom Kollek was largely an unknown. There was no time for weighing options; a decision was needed within the hour. Chouraqui, who had only recently stepped down from a demanding role in public office, agreed to Kollek's invitation. Kollek and Chouraqui were victorious in the October elections, and André became deputy mayor of Jerusalem. "We had to deal with all the same problems as every city hall in the world, but with a double handicap: we were in Israel, and it was Jerusalem that we were dealing with."[131]

In his capacity as deputy mayor, Chouraqui was given the special portfolios of cultural affairs and interreligious matters, roles in which his earlier life experience and fluency in Arabic proved to be considerable assets. From his city-hall office, he would be at the center of Jerusalem life through some of the city's most critical and bloodiest moments, notably the Six-Day War in June 1967 that recaptured East Jerusalem and reunited the city, and the 1973 Arab-Israeli War in October of that year. He writes with particular poignancy of the emotions stirred up by the city's reunification—the boundless rejoicing of its Jewish inhabitants, able once more to pray at the Western Wall, and the despair and fearfulness of some of its Arab citizens, for whom the defeat was a particularly bitter blow. And yet he also highlights personal stories of trust and reconciliation, of friendships renewed and property restored:

> We felt as though we were living out an incredible dream: in the dazzling light of spring, we were discovering with our own eyes the eastern part of Jerusalem which, for two decades, we had dreamed about, but without ever believing that that dream would someday become a reality.[132]

A man of three worlds

On 14 June 1967, the day of Pentecost, Jerusalem was invaded by pilgrims, not only from across the country, but from around the whole world, renewing a tradition that had been interrupted with the destruction of the Temple 1817 years earlier. The spirit of Pentecost was visibly present in the hearts of that multitude of men, women and children who, since our return from 102 countries of the world, had come for this timeless gathering, to kiss this Wall of Jubilation, which had become their stone fiancée. For 19 years, we had been climbing up on the rooftops of Mount Zion to see that inaccessible city with our own eyes. And now we were there, thinking that we were living out a dream that had taken two millennia to fulfil. It seemed as if the Wall had itself become a prayer for those among its people who had forgotten what praying meant.[133]

The Hebrew part of Jerusalem provided a paradoxical spectacle: that of a city abandoned by its Jewish population, which at that time was walking through the Arab part of the city. In our streets, Arabs were discovering with astonishment—and not without some shock—what the Jews had done on their side of the city. Curious onlookers were gathered at intersections to admire the traffic signals, which they had never seen before. Art-lovers rushed to the museums, and merchants rushed to the shops to compare prices. Everyone was dressed in their very best, and a festive atmosphere reigned throughout the city.... After twenty years apart, elderly people found each other once more, in the city's squares and streets and houses. Jews sought out Arab merchants in the Old City, to whom they owed small amounts which, since 1948, they had been unable to repay; those repayments brought joy to everyone. Arabs, carrying heavy suitcases in hand, sought out their former Jewish neighbors, to return possessions to them that had been faithfully guarded for two decades.

Once more, Jewish families found a daughter, or an aunt, or a cousin who had married an Arab, and had been living in the Old City. Throughout that day, and through the days afterward, there was not a single incident.[134]

Chouraqui's eight years in municipal politics were, as he himself described, a blend of triumphs and heartbreak, of idealistic vision and often frustrating bureaucracy and incomprehension. In the wake of the 1967 war, he penned his provocative and still-influential *Lettre à un ami arabe* (Letter to an Arab friend), which gained him a reputation among more hard-headed Israelis as hopelessly naive and politically unrealistic. As he himself commented with sad irony, "We have knocked down the concrete wall. But it will be more difficult to demolish the invisible wall which still separates Jews, Christians and Muslims in Jerusalem."[135] Nevertheless, he continued to hold out for the possibility of peaceful coexistence between Israel and its Arab neighbors, and, in 1967, was one of the founders of the Fraternité d'Abraham, one of the first national interfaith groups in France to bring together leaders of the Jewish, Muslim, and Christian faiths. Chouraqui was the first municipal leader to gather the heads of Jerusalem's religious communities together to discuss their needs, and to explore possible areas of collaboration; it was an unprecedented meeting, and occasioned a little discomfort (and some curiosity) on the part of the attendees:

> As the person on the municipal council who was responsible for inter-community, interreligious, and foreign relations for the city, as soon as calm had returned, I invited all the Christian and Muslim religious communities to gather at city hall. It was the first time in the history of Jerusalem that such a meeting had taken place; the ghettoization of the city had been almost complete. On the Christian side, there were delegations from eleven different denominations which, for the most part, did not even have relations with each other. Between Christians and Muslims, the separation was even more complete. We

were meeting the heads of these communities for the first time but, paradoxically, it was also the first time that the majority of them had met each other in the context of a friendly gathering. I told them that this was their city hall, and that it—and all the services it could provide—was at their service to help them in resolving their municipal problems. I noticed the effect on the Mea Shearim rabbis of so many priests and nuns, imams and cadis [who had responded to] this peaceful city invitation. Old Rabbi Pourush seemed fascinated by the nuns, whom he approached for the first time up close: "Oh, if only the daughters of Israel would dress as chastely as those sisters!" he said to me, with a glimmer of envy in his eyes.[136]

Among Chouraqui's final acts as deputy mayor was to visit the bereaved families of Israeli soldiers killed in the 1973 war, to extend the condolences of the city and offer its support to the survivors. Later that same year, he would reflect on the history and vocation of the Holy City in his book *Vivre pour Jérusalem* (Living for Jerusalem).

THE GENESIS OF *LA BIBLE CHOURAQUI*

Chouraqui's potent experiences of two eventful terms in Jerusalem politics left him exhausted, and perhaps somewhat disillusioned. In 1973, he stepped down permanently from elected office to dedicate himself to two initiatives that were particularly close to his heart: the urgent promotion of interreligious dialogue and understanding, and preparing a new translation of the Bible, which would enable him to apply the ideas and reflections culled over a lifetime of fascination with, and study of, this book:

I thirsted for silence. Stepping away from political life, freed from all my official roles, I could better devote myself to the translation of the Bible, as well as spreading the ideas that my recent books had been defending—my ceaseless appeals throughout the world for peace among the children of Abraham.[137]

It was around this same time that Chouraqui's friend Jacques Deschanel (an editorial director at Éditions Desclée) proposed that André prepare his own translation of the entire Hebrew Bible. It was not the first time such a suggestion had been made; twenty years earlier, following upon the success of Chouraqui's translations of the Psalms and the Song of Songs, French historian Jacques Madaule had made a similar request, which Chouraqui had declined at the time, feeling himself unready for such a major undertaking. But now, in his mid-fifties, rooted in the land of the Bible and with a wealth of time newly at his disposal, he decided to take up the project, and did so with astonishing vigor and single-mindedness.

This new and close-up familiarity with the Bible was bound up with an acute sense that everything he had lived through had been preparing him for this task: the polyglot nature of Algeria; the French language's rigor and stylistic elegance; what he had learned at the École rabbinique; the long periods meditating on the Bible and the Qur'an together with Jews, Christians, and Muslims; his retreat times spent in seminaries or deep in the Sahara desert; and, finally, his encounter with Hebrew, and with the landscapes where so much of the Bible had occurred—as living realities and no longer as mere book learning.

In twenty-eight months, between April 10, 1972, and August 14, 1974, André Chouraqui wrote out by hand, in black ink, the first draft of his complete initial translation of the three parts of the Hebrew Bible (the Pentateuch, the Prophets, the Writings), and of the four Gospels (which he titled "The Four Announcements"). Alone, over a period of two years, Chouraqui translated texts that had matured in the Middle East over more than a millennium and forged modern Judeo-Christian consciousness. Through his emphasis on unifying translations of key vocabulary terms and concepts, he underscored the profound unity of these texts. Once he had typed them up (since personal computers were unknown at the time), the typescripts were sent to specialists who revised, annotated, and critiqued them. Then Chouraqui went back to work, reviewing the text, sending it on to other specialists and tweaking it further. The first edition of the Hebrew Bible and the New Testament appeared in twenty-six volumes, between 1974 and 1977, published by Desclée de Brouwer. The text was published on its own, without any commentary, separated into volumes that (for the Hebrew Scriptures) employed once more the titles by which they were known in the Jewish tradition: one volume for Genesis (which became *Entête* [At-the-head], translating the Hebrew *Bereishit*), one for Exodus (*The Names*, from the Hebrew *Shemot*), and so on.

Throughout 1977, Chouraqui traveled throughout the Middle East and Europe, introducing and explaining his new translation, and the principles underlying it. In October, he was delighted to be able to present his twenty-six-volume set to Pope Paul VI, who commented that "it must have taken a great deal of love to succeed in such a task." In March 1978, Israeli President Katsir hosted a state reception, at which Chouraqui's translation was publicly presented, introduced by prominent biblical scholars. The level of interest and praise, among exegetes and the general public, was both surprising and affirming; within a few weeks of its publication, the first printing had already sold out.

Although he was formally retired from political life, throughout the 1970s, Chouraqui's personal prestige and his status as a high-ranking Arabic-speaking Israeli diplomat meant that he continued to be involved in semiofficial efforts toward peace and reconciliation in the Middle East. These included in-depth personal discussions with Morocco's King Hassan II in 1977, at the conclusion of which the king—at Chouraqui's request—authorized the Chouraquis' Israeli passports to be stamped with an exit visa when they left the kingdom. Very likely, it was the first time an Israeli passport was recognized at the border of an Arab country. He also engaged in behind-the-scenes work to promote the peace negotiations that culminated in the Camp David Accords between Egypt and Israel, which were eventually signed by Prime Minister Menachem Begin, President Anwar Sadat,

Une Vie Très Pleine

and President Jimmy Carter on March 26, 1979. To Chouraqui, diplomacy was an important way in which he sought to live out his guiding spiritual vision and convictions. The religious and the political went together.

On December 24, 1977, Chouraqui was stunned to hear Israeli radio announcers claiming that he was slated to be named the next president of Israel. Apparently, Menachem Begin was seeking a distinguished Sephardic Jew to accept the honorary position and, without consulting Chouraqui, government sources had begun to quietly leak the news of his nomination, to gauge public reaction. Some Jewish religious groups raised concerns about the candidacy of a man who had such an obvious affinity for both Christians and Muslims. Although his wife Annette did not pressure him one way or the other, André sensed that his own political and social views would put him at odds with the vision espoused by the Begin government. Chouraqui let it be known that, as honored as he was to be nominated, his biblical translation work required his undivided attention, and that he had no desire to assume yet another official post. In the end, the position was given instead to Yitzhak Navon, another Maghrebin Jew and former political secretary to David Ben-Gurion.

The 1970s and 1980s were a fruitful and busy time for Chouraqui. He was increasingly sought out to give lectures around the world on religious, biblical, and political subjects. In 1979, he published his first "intellectual autobiography," *Ce que je crois* ("What I believe," translated as *A Man in Three Worlds*), and met with the recently elected Pope John Paul II, urging the Holy See's recognition of the State of Israel—a long-time hope of Chouraqui's that would eventually be realized with the December 1993 "Fundamental Agreement" between the two states. The year 1979 also marked the beginning of negotiations with the Brépols publishing house, to issue a deluxe edition of *La Bible Chouraqui*; this would eventually become Chouraqui's ten-volume magnum opus, *L'Univers de la Bible* (The world of the Bible).

Colette, André's first wife, had never ceased to be an intimate spiritual presence in his life. In the autumn of 1981, she fell gravely ill—her final sickness in a long life of suffering. Providentially, André was in France at the time and, advised of her condition, immediately went to be with her at her home in Lourdes. For the last few days of her life, André read her passages from her beloved Hebrew Bible; she died in his arms on October 15, ending a long, loving, but deeply conflicted relationship. André assisted at her burial, praying the Kaddish and the traditional Psalms for a Jewish funeral.

In the autumn of 1982, the first of the ten volumes of *L'Univers de la Bible* came off the presses of Éditions Brépols. It was a magnificent coffee-table edition, lavishly illustrated with pictures selected by museum curators and biblical archaeologists to elucidate the history and culture of biblical times. Unlike the earlier editions, this version incorporated extensive editorial notes, exploring the meaning of the text and unpacking Chouraqui's own translational choices. Extensive sidebars throughout the text exposed his readers to Jewish, Muslim, and Christian traditions of interpreting key biblical stories and characters. In *L'Univers de la Bible*, Chouraqui sought to combine aspects of a traditional study Bible, a commentary, and an introduction to the biblical commonalities and differences of the three Abrahamic faiths. In the spring of 1983, Chouraqui would be invited to present a copy of the first volume in the set to French President François Mitterand.

In 1984, Chouraqui's career as a translator took a new but unsurprising turn: given his lifelong familiarity with Arabic (his mother tongue), he set out to prepare his own French translation of the Qur'an, to complete his work on the Abrahamic scriptures. The publishing schedule of *L'Univers de la Bible* continued apace, with volume 10 of *L'Univers de la Bible* finally appearing at the end of 1985, marking the completion of Chouraqui's truly monumental *ouvrage*—three thousand full-color photos, and roughly twenty million typeset letters, in a format that was vaguely reminiscent of traditional rabbinic Bibles (*Miqraot Gedolot*) and the glossed Bibles of medieval Christianity. The year was brought to a historic finish with a Vatican press conference presenting his work (December 11) and a private audience (December 12) with Pope John Paul II, during which

Une Vie Très Pleine

Chouraqui presented the pontiff with a set of *L'Univers de la Bible*, as well as a memorandum regarding the establishment of diplomatic relations between the Holy See and the State of Israel. Both the French and Israeli embassies in Rome hosted diplomatic receptions in Chouraqui's honor. Chouraqui's reputation as an author was matched by his profile as a lecturer much in demand at colloquia around the world, and as a frequent media commentator on Middle Eastern affairs.

ÉMINENCE GRISE

As Chouraqui entered his seventies, his literary output showed no signs of slowing. In 1990, his second autobiography, *L'Amour fort comme la mort* (Love as strong as death), was published by Éditions Robert Laffont; it would sell more than 100,000 copies and would subsequently be republished twice. At the end of 1990, his new translation of the Qur'an was finally published, making him the first person in modern history—likely *all* of history—to have translated, largely on his own, the scriptures of the three Abrahamic faiths. Roughly eighteen years had passed since he first undertook the project of translating the entire Bible, and Chouraqui was now firmly established as one of the most noteworthy biblical translators and commentators in the modern world. Awards from the Sorbonne, the University of Louvain, and the Evangelical University of Tübingen confirmed his status in academic circles; once again, a series of lectures, interviews, and appearances on radio and television followed in quick succession. In March 1992, he published his analysis of the diplomatic and religious challenges between Israel and the Vatican in a new book called *La reconnaissance: le Saint-Siège, les Juifs et Israël* (Recognition: The Holy See, the Jews and Israel). The book was published at a critical moment and proved to be prophetic in its push for mutual diplomatic relations, which were, in fact, established less than two years later, on December 30, 1993.

On December 15, 1994, at the Élysée Palace, Chouraqui was honored by the French Republic, when President François Mitterrand inducted him into the French Legion of Honor, with the rank of commander. It must have been a particularly bittersweet occasion for a man who had always taken such pride in his French identity, but who had never forgotten the pain of being summarily disowned by France during the war. On October 3 of that same year, André suffered a severe stroke, but was eventually able to return to his home and recommence his schedule of activities. On December 18, the city of Jerusalem conferred its highest municipal honor on Chouraqui, naming him *Yakir Yerushalayim*, "Worthy [Citizen] of Jerusalem/ Treasured Jerusalemite."

Despite a punishing schedule of lectures, interviews, and conference interventions, Chouraqui did not abandon his intellectual, literary, and translational activity. He edited *Chronique de Baba: Lettres d'Abraham Meyer* (Baba's chronicle: The Letters of Abraham Meyer), a series of eighty letters written in Judeo-Arabic by his grandfather during the First World War, as well as a Hebrew commentary on Psalm 119 that had been composed by his distinguished ancestor Saadia Chouraqui in Algeria in the seventeenth century. *Ton étoile et ta croix* (Your cross and your star), the chronicle of his extraordinary relationship with his first wife and "spiritual sister" Colette, would be published in 1998, incorporating extensive excerpts from their decades-long correspondence.

Despite his age, Chouraqui did not desist from traveling widely, frequently speaking to political and religious colloquia around the world, being interviewed by the international press, and actively pursuing his work in favor of interreligious harmony and cooperation. In May of 2001, he published his third and final autobiographical work, *Mon testament: Le feu de l'Alliance* (My testament: The fire of the covenant), in which he deftly wove together the experiences of a long and remarkable life, and the insights he had gleaned from decades of study and translation of the Abrahamic scriptures. To Chouraqui's mind, it would be his philosophical legacy to the world. Although his writing career was now largely behind him, his earlier volumes continued to be reprinted, and to be translated into more than twenty languages, including Russian and Japanese, extending the scope of his influence to a readership that was by this point literally worldwide. In

Une Vie Très Pleine

March 2007, *Le destin d'Israël* was published, a fascinating selection from sixty years of Chouraqui's discussions and correspondence with major twentieth-century religious and cultural figures, including Jules Isaac, Jacques Ellul, Marc Chagall, Jacques Maritain, and Paul Claudel.

MORT DE JOIE

Le destin d'Israël was to be the last of Chouraqui's books he would live to see published. In the early hours of July 9, 2007, after several months of declining health, André Chouraqui died peacefully at his home in Jerusalem, surrounded by his family, and, in accordance with Jewish tradition, was buried later the same day. His interment was attended by family members and friends, but it was perhaps most indicative of the character of the man that the mourners included not only France's chief rabbi-emeritus, René-Samuel Sirat, but also Chouraqui's friends and colleagues from the Christian community, including Father Émile Shoufani of Nazareth, and Brother Yohanan Elihai, a Little Brother of Jesus (of Charles de Foucauld), who, born Jean Leroy, had taken on a new Hebrew identity in 1960, and had remained one of Chouraqui's dearest and oldest friends. Chouraqui's gravestone was engraved (as he had earlier requested in *L'Amour fort comme la mort*) with an inscription that began with the words *Mort de joie* (loosely, "I have died of joy").

Chouraqui's death brought an outpouring of praise and tributes, moving personal testimonials from friends and former political colleagues, and noteworthy obituaries in many major newspapers. In a letter to Madame Chouraqui, French President Nicolas Sarkozy was eloquent in his praise of the deceased scholar and *homme de la politique*, whom he described as "the great writer and humanist André Chouraqui":

> The work that your husband has left for posterity is of major importance. He played a major role in the *rapprochement* of the three monotheistic religions, inspired as he was by his passion for brotherhood. His translation

of the Hebrew Bible and the New Testament are...the legacy of a humanistic intellectual, to whom people searching for spirituality will continue to refer.[138]

Israeli President Shimon Peres, who had known Chouraqui for decades and had frequently worked alongside him in political life, called him "a great leader, a great writer, and a great citizen of Jerusalem." Similar tributes were addressed to Annette and their family from the dizzyingly broad spectrum of Chouraqui's colleagues, friends, and admirers: the rector of the Islamic Institute at Paris's Mosque; the Alliance Israélite Universelle, whose tireless ambassador André had been for decades; the Benedictine Monastery of Maredsous, renowned for its translations and study of the Bible; French Jesuit colleagues; and from Jewish-Christian and other interreligious organizations throughout Europe and around the world. These letters attested both to Chouraqui's qualities as an individual, and to the broad impact of his literary work, his political career, and his interreligious engagements.

The London *Times*'s obituary, published on August 8, 2007, spoke glowingly of Chouraqui's dedication to building bridges between faiths and highlighted the uniqueness and value of his translations in fostering that goal:

> Chouraqui's passion for building bridges between the three monotheistic faiths was kindled during his childhood spent in Algeria....In the aftermath [of the 1967 war], Chouraqui sought to recreate in Jerusalem the links between Muslims and Jews he had enjoyed in his Algerian childhood. His success was inevitably limited and he decided that he could serve his cause better as a writer. "I am a scribe and I am a linguist," he insisted. "I am neither a politician, nor a theologian."[139]

In his obituary written for *Le Monde*, Chouraqui's colleague and fellow translator Henri Tincq referred to him as a "juggler of words and sounds," and underscored the eclecticism of Chouraqui's

Une Vie Très Pleine

life and literary output, as well as the way in which his childhood experiences had shaped his vision of dialogue as an adult:

> It was from his parents' Algeria that André Chouraqui drew his genius for languages, and his mad dream of peace among the three monotheistic religions. Born in Aïn Témouchent to a father who was a vintner and merchant, with ancestors who had come from Spain and adopted Arab culture, he spoke Arabic with his Muslim friends, French to his family, and Hebrew in the synagogue. "Three languages, three sacred texts, three religions and three cultures were constantly swirling around in my head," he was fond of saying, concerning his childhood....
>
> In 1972, he began to translate the Bible, living in the land where it was born, by hewing as closely as possible to its original language, its rhythm, its vocabulary, its musicality, which gave rise to Chouraqui's reputation as esoteric.... His effort consisted in finding once more the genuineness of the Bible, and his underlying intuition, which was a blend of sensitivity to transcendence and unity. He restored the power of God's name—*Adonai-Elohims*—revealed to Moses in the Burning Bush, but then translated (and betrayed) from Olympus to the Aventine Hill, using the names of local deities: *Dieu*, which is derived from the Latin *deus*, which is linked to the name Zeus, and the Greek *theos*. Just as *God* is a form of Tor and Wotan, Nordic deities.
>
> André Chouraqui—a juggler of words and sounds—also set to work on the translation of the Gospels and, in 1977, the 26 volumes of his Hebrew Bible and New Testament appeared. Alongside this colossal task, he kept up his work as a historian, exegete, essayist and poet. Eclectic and bulimic, Chouraqui published works on the State of Israel, on Theodor Herzl, on the history of Judaism, on the rebirth of contemporary Judaism, and then the eight volumes of *L'Univers de la Bible*, books of poetry, a play (*The Trial of*

Jesus), and then *Jesus and Paul: Sons of Israel, What I Believe*, etc.

His translation only makes sense within the framework of the brotherhood of the People of the Book to which he always aspired, first in Paris and later on in Jerusalem.... Unquestioned specialists in the Qur'an congratulated him, but fundamentalists were scandalized. Christian fundamentalists had reacted the same way when this Jew embarked on translating the Gospel of Christ.

This was the first time that one man had translated all three holy books. Each word of them was chosen, was chiseled out according to a fearful type of intellectual gymnastics. It was a work that was, at the same time, an act of faith in understanding among the three religions—but he had a particular passion for reconciliation between Jews and Christians....

Despite the handicap of his leg, which slowed him down his whole life long, André Chouraqui leaves behind him the memory of a pilgrim of the covenant of cultures and religions, a memory which remains alive on every road in the world, from Brazil to Japan, and in all of the countries which make up Europe and Africa.[140]

France's minister of culture, Christine Albanel, described Chouraqui as "one of the consciences of our century, an eminent figure of both the Hebrew and French cultures...an admirable ambassador of the French language, which he employed for the most beautiful of tasks: exalting spirituality, brotherhood and peace among peoples."[141] The Swiss newspaper *Le Temps* admitted that his version was "an abrupt text which overturned all the usual translational expectations, and mangled French syntax," and yet "it is shot through with a poetic power and a freshness that other translations do not have."[142] Dr. Yohanan Elihai, a distinguished French-Israeli linguist and interreligious pioneer who first met André in October 1948, did not shy away from both the *strengths* and the *weaknesses* of Chouraqui's translational undertaking:

> André's contribution will be through his translations, which kept close to the Hebrew (and are sometimes clunky, and even a bit far-fetched…one may not agree with him here and there), and especially through his typographic convention [Y$_\text{H W}^\text{ADONAÏ}$H], which awakened French-speaking Christians, and got them to adopt the Jewish tradition in this regard, that attitude of great respect—I dare say, of adoration—that one can adopt when they encounter this YHWH.[143]

Around the globe, Chouraqui's death was marked with sadness for the loss of the man—but also with profound respect and gratitude for the legacy he had bequeathed to the world: the example of concrete, tireless action to promote interreligious dialogue, to penetrate more deeply into the multiple layers of biblical meaning, and to create a world in which the biblical message was not only *read* and *studied*, but could truly be the template for modern political, social, and economic life. Chouraqui combined an idealistic vision with a profound, lived awareness of the best and worst of humanity, an optimism tempered by the realism of the trenches—but which, however, never degenerated for him into either pessimism or negativity.

Chouraqui's work cannot really be separated from his own singular personal history, and the constellation of events and experiences in which he found himself. It was because of France's colonial presence in his native Algeria that André Chouraqui first encountered European Christians and Christian culture. Those Christian contacts, beginning with the local Catholic kindergarten he attended, continued through his life in Paris, and kindled in him a fascination with Christianity. The experience of the war years raised painful questions for him about the motivation for collaborationist Christians, and for the widespread apathy in the face of Jewish suffering, and yet also spurred him to work with pioneering figures like Jules Isaac, to build bridges with like-minded Christians. He believed in a better, different future, and he labored passionately to bring that future about.

Chouraqui was fortunate to live in an era when Jewish-Christian reconciliation was the order of the day, but also in which Christians themselves were experiencing a new desire to rediscover Judaism and the "Jewish roots" of Christianity for themselves. The postwar *glasnost* between Jews and Christians produced Christians who actively sought out and studied Jewish sources in their research, and who engaged in scholarly dialogue with Jewish experts. International colloquia, and local interfaith dialogue initiatives, encouraged a thawing of the traditional "chill" between the two religions and established a critical mass of individuals—both on the scholarly and popular levels—for whom Judaism was no longer a relative "unknown," but a dynamic, living conversation partner, both enriching and challenging traditional Christian interpretations and categories. The Romanian-born Israeli scholar Bluma Finkelstein (herself profoundly skeptical of the concept and motives of "Jewish-Christian dialogue") nevertheless acknowledges that the postwar era created a very new situation, both psychologically and theologically, for Jews and Christians alike:

> At this end of the twentieth century…a part of the Christian world—conscious of its share of responsibility for Nazism, needed this dialogue with the Jews, in order to beat its breast. Europe's Jews—the survivors who had to continue living in a Christian setting—also needed an acknowledgement from the segment of the Christian world that was repenting. Each side was trying to exorcise its own demons. At that moment there appeared a factor that was entirely new in the twentieth century: Jewish writers. For the first time, really, Jewish intellectuals spoke up, and dared to say out loud, and without hesitation, what they thought of Christianity and Christians. They took it upon themselves to be spokespersons for the Jewish people, and for the Jewish religion. Some of them

Une Vie Très Pleine

were more nuanced in their critiques, either out of conviction or out of a desire to build a bridge between the two communities, whatever the cost. Such was the case for Jules Isaac, and André Chouraqui after him. Others, such as Emmanuel Lévinas, Edmond Fleg or Arnold Mandel, simply expressed the traditional Jewish (that is, Orthodox) point-of-view.[144]

In such a changed world, it now became not only thinkable but desirable for a Jewish scholar to embark on a translation of the New Testament—a momentous and still radical idea—and the ground was prepared for its reception in Christian and Jewish circles. A quarter century after World War II, the 1970s and 1980s marked a time when a Jewish scholar could translate the Christian Scriptures without the need to apologize, and when Christians were open to the unique contributions that Jewish scholarship could offer to an accurate and informed understanding of their own faith. In so many ways, it was a particularly propitious historical moment, and André Chouraqui would seem to be the ideal person to engage in such a venture, breaking new ground in the reading of an age-old religious text.

Because of the extreme variety and rich fabric of his life, André Chouraqui remains a difficult man to categorize or label. He was, in many senses, an authentic "Renaissance man," actively involved in a broad range of disciplines, a man who saw literature, politics, and religion as deeply and necessarily intermeshed, and who, in his own life, allowed each to freely influence the others. He was unquestionably a "man of the Book," a "man of the Land," and a "man of his people." But that "people" was always larger for him than simply Israel or Judaism, larger than his Algerian roots or his profound insertion into French intellectual life. Without ever renouncing his faith or his culture, he nevertheless succeeded in being an eminent member of the larger "family of Abraham," showing humanity that identity need not mean chauvinism, that faith need not imply prejudice, and that the deepest currents of the authentically religious heart would

A man of three worlds

always seek what they shared in common, rather than what divided them. It was a profound lesson for the twentieth century. It's to be hoped that his example and writings can provide a similar impetus for such thinking and acting in this twenty-first century—and perhaps beyond.

אַשְׁרֵי רֹדְפֵי שָׁלוֹם כִּי־ בְנֵי אֱלֹהִים יִקָּרֵא לָהֶם
Blessed are the pursuers of peace, for they will be called God's children.

(Matthew 5:9, literal translation from Delitzsch's Hebrew New Testament; see Psalm 34:14)

EPILOGUE

Chouraqui's legacy

André Chouraqui's death in the summer of 2007 sadly extinguished a remarkable literary, political, cultural—and especially interreligious—life. But it did not bring an end to Chouraqui's impact, or his inspiring personal legacy. The years since his death have confirmed the prescience of many of his instincts and have seen his ideas built and expanded upon by other scholars, by friends, and by those who see value in the interfaith vision that he tirelessly advocated. There is today an association, Les Amis d'André Chouraqui (The friends of André Chouraqui), that continues to share and promote his vision.

Most of Chouraqui's life was lived in the decades *before* 9/11, those dramatic events that brought Islam (and dialogue with Islam) to the forefront of Western consciousness. Many of us can remember how, in the days and weeks afterward, local mosques and Islamic cultural centers opened their doors to their neighbors in new ways, seeking to counter the violent version of jihad linked to Osama Bin Laden and his followers. We remember the goodwill of many non-Muslims, who set out to learn more about Islam and the Qur'an, and we recall politicians who sought to carefully distinguish the faith of Muslims worldwide from the destructive ideology espoused and rationalized by some in the name of Islam. We remember George W. Bush's famous words on September 17, 2001: "The face of terror is not the true faith of Islam. That's not what Islam is all about. Islam is

Epilogue

peace....When we think of Islam we think of a faith that brings comfort to a billion people around the world....[Muslims] need to be treated with respect."[145]

For his entire adult life, André Chouraqui tried to find ways for three of the world's great monotheistic faiths—Judaism, Christianity, and Islam—to view one another differently, beyond the clichés and stereotypes of their pasts. Interfaith dialogue today is an established, respected form of civic engagement, and it grows, year by year, throughout our world. But it was not always so widespread. In the 1970s, country music legend Glen Campbell sang "I knew Jesus before he was a superstar"; in a similar vein, André Chouraqui was passionate about interfaith bridge building long before it became mainstream and cool. Even before the term *interfaith* itself began to be widely used (which, according to the Oxford English Dictionary, was around 1967), André Chouraqui was *doing* it.

In France, in Israel, and around the world, Chouraqui helped to found, and to foster, organizations that could bring the children of Abraham together in peaceful coexistence and fruitful exchange. What is today a commonplace of our world was still relatively rare during the first half of Chouraqui's life. Conversations that he had with Jules Isaac toward the end of World War II, and circles of like-minded religious leaders that he was part of, are undeniably some of the roots of today's interreligious worldview. Interfaith organizations he helped to establish are still flourishing today. Although some of the impetus for contemporary dialogue among faiths comes from ground-shaking modern events like 9/11, it is important to remember those (like Chouraqui) who were doing it more than half a century earlier, and whose enthusiasm for that vision never flagged. It was his work, and the work of people like him, that *made* it mainstream and kept it before the eyes of the world's religious and political leaders. Their tenacity, their creative forms of outreach, and their faith proved transformative...and we are *all* the beneficiaries of their efforts—and those who are challenged to continue that momentum in a changed, and changing, world.

As we look back over his life and work, three aspects of Chouraqui's biblical translation project stand out today as particularly prophetic and of lasting value:

1. his respectfully iconoclastic mode of translation: the refreshing new renderings he offers, injecting new life into these classic texts and challenging readers to hear them differently (and to think differently about them);
2. his effort to highlight the linguistic roots (and root meanings) of many common biblical terms, and to reveal linguistic characteristics that other translations may have underplayed;
3. his emphasis on the Jewishnesss of Jesus as a necessary "interpretive key" for the Gospels, and one that could ultimately bring Jews and Christians together in conversation.

REBEL TRANSLATOR

In his first goal, Chouraqui's work ranks alongside other translations that sought to "jar" their readers into new ways of understanding through a rugged translational style and unfamiliar wordings. English versions like *The Cotton Patch Gospels* (prepared by Southern Baptist minister Clarence Jordan between 1968 and 1973) and, more recently, the "Good As New" translation (published in 2004 by John Henson, a somewhat atypical British Baptist), set out to express the Bible's ancient message in radically idiomatic language that can speak, directly and compellingly, to modern readers. Chouraqui did not shy away from using—and inventing—vocabulary that frequently made his readers scratch their heads (but which, he hoped, would ultimately reward their efforts with valuable new insights). His goal was to "shake up" the status quo in biblical translation and study.

There can be no question that he did that in the French-speaking world. Chouraqui's version frequently makes people stumble; they are forced to read and *re*-read, to struggle and to dig, in order to appreciate the not-always-obvious points he is trying to make. At first reading, it is not an easy translation to grasp. For some, this has led more deeply and profitably into the Bible's multiple layers of meaning; for others, it has proven so dense, confusing, and impenetrable that they were ultimately *turned off* the Bible. For as many as were intrigued and enlightened by Chouraqui, there were countless others for whom his style was either a distraction or an obstacle. As the Latin proverb says, *de gustibus non est disputandum*; there is no point in debating about taste. While Chouraqui's version has great value for some readers, it is not necessarily suited to everyone (as, of course, can be said of *every* translation of the Bible). It is, admittedly, something of an acquired taste, but it rewards those who are willing to cheer its translator on in his theological and linguistic wrestling match.

POLYGLOT WORDSMITH

Chouraqui's passion for etymology, and his desire to mine the linguistic riches of words and concepts, has enlightened many but has also certainly confused others. His approach has had the benefit of bringing to the surface the "unvarnished" origins of biblical terms, often highlighting facets of their meaning that were traditionally either hidden or downplayed as unnecessary. His research has sparked new inquiries into apparently "settled" interpretations, and he has enabled readers without extensive training in biblical languages to appreciate the nuances and playfulness in those ancient texts.

But as his critics correctly charged, many of those nuances only really make sense to those who are already comfortable in Hebrew or Greek, who are able to appreciate the arguments he makes, and follow the logic of his conclusions. To most fully appreciate Chouraqui's reasoning, it's necessary to have access to the extensive explanatory notes in his deluxe translation-commentary, *L'Univers de la Bible*, where the translation is unpacked at length (unfortunately, that edition has been out of print for more than thirty years, and is not widely available). Without it, the text can seem quirky, esoteric, and unintelligible at best, pedantic or pretentious at worst. While Chouraqui's extensive knowledge of languages permits him to draw on interesting linguistic trivia and make provocative juxtapositions, on a few occasions, Chouraqui's enthusiasm seems to have outrun his prudent judgement, and other scholars have pointed to questionable interpretations, or outright errors, among his linguistic conclusions. Biblical terminology has not always had the same meaning over many centuries, and the exact relationship of Jesus's (Hebrew? Aramaic?) words to our Gospels in Greek continues to spark debate. But it is a debate that Chouraqui would be happy to see taking place.

For these reasons, some of Chouraqui's most interesting intuitions will likely need to remain at the level of conjecture and discussion...but he has certainly opened doors for the work of future scholars in these fields that may yield further confirmation of ideas he first put forward. Chouraqui was a consummate intellectual, but at times, he may seem to overthink mundane issues, and "read into" the text meanings that go well beyond the intention or knowledge of the original human authors. For religious believers, however, no detail in the text is too inconsequential to be potentially revelatory, and nothing is random, arbitrary, or deprived of meaning. Chouraqui's close, loving reading of the biblical text—in a profoundly *Jewish* way—certainly invites modern readers to engage with the Bible with similar creativity, imagination, and with all of the wonderful analytical tools at our disposal today. What he does *not* want is for people to simply skim over words they *assume* they understand, without pausing to really *chew over* them, doing justice to both their linguistic and theological heft.

A JEW...FOR JESUS

Chouraqui's determination to underscore Jesus's full insertion into the religion and culture of his people has been confirmed in spades over the last forty years by shelves full of scholarly and popular books and articles. "The Jewishness of Jesus" is now so programmatic in both historical and theological studies that it seems hard to believe that it was ever otherwise. But that foundational insight has only spawned new questions: *What type of a Jew* was Jesus (within the spectrum of first-century Jewish religious and political groups we know about)? What was the relationship of Jewish faith and Hellenistic culture in the Galilee in which he grew up? How do recent archaeological discoveries (such as those at Sepphoris, Capharnaum, Nazareth, and Magdala) throw important light on everyday life and religious practice—and how might those discoveries inform and nuance our understandings of Jesus and the Gospels? In what ways were Judean and Galilean Judaism lived out similarly (and differently), and how does this geography impact the story of Jesus? The postwar development of positive Jewish-Christian relations means that there is today a large and growing pool of Jewish experts actively involved in researching and discussing issues linked to the Gospels, and of Christian scholars who have studied Judaism and Jewish texts in-depth (often at Jewish institutions). Chouraqui would almost certainly be thrilled to know that there is today a *Jewish Annotated New Testament* and dozens of prominent Jewish academics interested in early Christianity. This has led to a fertile collaboration and unprecedented intellectual cross-pollination that will yield further insights in coming years and decades. For Christians who see Jesus as the incarnation of God's presence, a more accurate reconstruction of that first-century Jewish world can only serve to enrich the multidimensionality of Jesus's life.

For Jewish scholars, scratching "beneath the surface" of Christian writings often yields a human Jesus who fits comfortably into ancient Jewish life, and who feels less and less like a stranger. This irenic shared learning and reflection is precisely what Chouraqui always wanted to facilitate, and he would no doubt be pleased to see the great strides that have already taken place. Seeds that he helped to sow, tentatively, decades ago, are today bearing rich fruit, for the benefit of those two faiths and, ultimately, for the benefit of the entire human race.

According to the story of the Tower of Babel, it was *language*, in the service of arrogance, that was at the root of the fragmentation of humanity; a shared language sought to exalt humanity to the level of the divine, with disastrous consequences.

Restoring the Gospel's Jewish Voice

Today, it is *also* language—in the service of listening, openness, and dialogue—that is helping to heal the tensions, pain, and injustices of nearly two thousand years. Wherever in the world Jews and Christians (and, increasingly, Muslims) are coming together to learn in common, they are discovering a shared language rooted in their history and their Scriptures. They are finding new ways to speak to, with, and about one another. *That* kind of shared language was precisely what André Chouraqui dreamed of; it was that vision that he wanted to ground in his unique translation of the Abrahamic holy books. His intellect, his life experience, and his indomitable optimism combined to produce a Bible version (and a translation of the Qur'an) that are as much *invitation* as *translation*. They dare their readers to embark on a journey that is both destabilizing and reassuring. And, while they certainly do not answer *every* question that Jews, Christians, and Muslims bring to their reading, there is one question they *do* answer: Can Christians, Muslims, and Jews find in their inspired texts the tools for building a hopeful and respectful future? André Chouraqui's answer is a resounding yes. Through *La Bible Chouraqui*, his yes continues to echo today, inviting us to continue the work he did, and to further the intellectual and personal legacy he has left us. Will we be up to the task? *Insh'Allah*, as Chouraqui's Arab-speaking Muslim friends would say…God willing.

> Ongoing contact with the Other no longer allows us to withdraw into ourselves. The Other is not just my neighbor in my village; he is also my most distant brother, at the other end of the world. All of the ghettos that human beings have built, in which they have mutually imprisoned each other, are no longer helpful; on the contrary, they are a threat. The modern world imposes the absolute need for us to come out of our ghettos; universality is the necessary condition for our survival.…If every human being were to open themselves up to the Other, then their life, the life of their family and of their community would be metamorphosed.
>
> (André Chouraqui)[146]

AFTERWORD

Dr. Eugene J. Fisher, Distinguished Professor, Saint Leo University

This is a book that will be of great interest to Jews and Christians, Catholic, Orthodox, and Protestant. Biblical scholars, historians, pastors, priests, and rabbis will learn many new things that will enrich and deepen their scholarly pursuits and, indeed, their personal, spiritual lives. It is well written and easy to read, not only by scholars but the average reader who wishes to deepen her or his understanding of Judaism and Christianity. Also, Muslims will be interested since Andre Chouraqui translated not only the Hebrew Scriptures/*TaNaCh* (Torah/*Neviiem*-Prophets/*Chetuvim*-Writings) but also the Qur'an. He was involved not only in Jewish-Christian dialogues in France, and around the world, but also in fostering Jewish/Christian/Muslim trialogues based on deepening the understanding of the sacred scriptures of the three Abrahamic faiths.

Chouraqui, born and raised in Algeria, spoke Arabic and French as a child. Moving to France, he studied both law and rabbinic studies, and during World War II fought against the Nazis as a resistance fighter, helping many Jews to hide and survive the Shoah/Holocaust. He became fluent in Hebrew when, later in life, he moved to Israel, also becoming a political leader in Jerusalem and fostering Jewish/Christian and Jewish/Christian/Muslim dialogues. This trifold interreligious experience illuminates his translations into French of the Bible and the Qur'an. Watson provides numerous examples of how Chouraqui's translations of the sacred texts of the three religions can both surprise readers and deepen our understanding of them, whatever our religious background.

Halfway through the book Watson distills his profound understanding of Chouraqui's writings: "I believe that the specific richness of Andre Chouraqui's work lies in its powers of reconciliation: religious faith with scientific inquiry; beauty with accuracy; antiquity with modernity; East with West; Jewish with Christian. The ability to achieve all of this has its foundation in the specificity of Chouraqui's religious, historical, geographical, and cultural vantage point." This is how, Watson notes, Chouraqui's scholarly, personal, spiritual, biblical, and dialogical passions "were forged." A unique life of love for the other.

Chouraqui centered his work on the Jewishness of Jesus/*Yeshua* and of the New Testament, which is a work written by Jews, about a Jew, for primarily Jewish readers. Christianity over the centuries took the New Testament out of its natural historical, cultural, and religious context and so ended up misunderstanding its true meaning and the full significance of the teachings of *Yeshua*/Jesus for the Jews of his own time and place and, therefore, for all times and places.

Watson understands Chouraqui, correctly, as "a man of three worlds," whose passion in life was to bring the three together in dialogue and understanding so that our interwoven faith communities can work, together, to right the wrongs we encounter in the world (*tikkun olam*—healing the world), to help those in need: the poor, the sick, the ignorant, and those looking for a purpose in their lives. This book will help all readers achieve those goals, personally and professionally.

I have personally been involved in Jewish-Christian relations for half a century since I earned my doctorate as pretty much the only Catholic studying at the Institute of Hebrew Studies at New York University. I went on to work for the U.S. Conference of Catholic Bishops in charge of its Secretariat for Catholic-Jewish relations and as a consultor to the Holy See, becoming involved in numerous meetings of the International Catholic-Jewish Relations Committee. During one meeting, I had the good fortune of meeting with Chouraqui, though I cannot say I got to know him well, as his deep friends such as Martin Buber, Franz Rosenzweig, and Albert Camus

Afterword

certainly did. Even with my deep background in studying the Hebrew Scriptures/*TaNaCh*, the New Testament, and, above all, Jewish-Christian relations, historically and theologically, I must admit that I learned a lot from this excellent book about Judaism and Christianity/Catholicism, both what we have in common and how our paths have diverged, and why.

Watson quotes Chouraqui's words at the end of World War II in Paris: "On the parvis in front of Notre Dame [Cathedral], I contemplated the statue representing the Synagogue, blindfolded, holding a broken sceptre, by the side of her triumphant sister, the Church.... Thirty-three centuries of Mosaic religion, two thousand years of Christianity, came to their climax in the bankruptcy of the Second World War." Chouraqui, I believe, would be heartened to note that a new statue of *Synagoga/Ecclesia* has been commissioned, in which the two sisters stand together, looking at each other in dialogue, holding together the scrolls of the Bible, discussing together what the Scriptures mean for Christians and Jews.

GLOSSARY

Adonai. Hebrew for "My Lord." A title of God used frequently in Jewish Scripture and prayer, especially to replace the Tetragrammaton (YHWH), which was considered so sacred as to be unpronounceable in daily life.

alterity. A philosophical and anthropological term for "otherness."

Aramaic. A Semitic language very similar to Hebrew, which became the common administrative language of much of the ancient Middle East, especially under the Assyrian and Persian Empires, between around 600 and 200 BCE. Small groups of Middle Eastern Christians continue to use Aramaic as their spoken and/or liturgical language. See **Common Era**.

Babylonian Talmud. The larger and later of the two classic collections of Jewish legal interpretation, largely in Aramaic, and compiled by scholars of Babylonian Jewish academies, around 600 CE. See also **Talmud**.

Berber. An ethnocultural group indigenous to Algeria and other parts of North and West Africa, descended from some of the pre-Islamic tribes in this region.

Chosen People. A religious concept in Judaism (and, to an extent, Christianity), according to which God, through their ancestors, chose the Jewish people as the recipients of a special covenantal relationship, to accomplish a special purpose in the history of salvation.

Cistercians, Order of. An austere Catholic religious order of monks and nuns, rooted in a medieval renewal of strict adherence to the Rule of St. Benedict. They are named for the French village (Cîteaux; in Latin, *Cistercium*) that became the center of their order.

cognate. A word related to another word on the basis of having the same linguistic derivation (from the Latin *cognatus*, "born together").

Common Era (CE; contrasts with Before Common Era, BCE). A system of dating used in many academic contexts today, considered more religiously neutral than the older (largely Christian) terminology AD (*anno Domini*; Latin for "in the year of the Lord"); the two systems correspond exactly.

Council of Chalcedon. A major Christian church council held in 451 CE, notable for issuing the Chalcedonian Definition of Jesus's full divinity and humanity: "We confess one and the same Son, who is our Lord Jesus Christ…complete in his deity and complete—the very same—in his humanity, truly God and truly a human being… coessential with the Father as to his deity and coessential with us as to his humanity, being like us in every respect apart from sin."

Crémieux decree. An 1870 French colonial legal decree conferring French citizenship on most Algerian Jews; it was revoked during the Second World War, under France's Vichy Régime.

dialogical. Related to or characterized by dialogue and its use.

dynamic equivalence. Term coined by linguist Eugene Nida to describe a translation approach that privileges readability in the language being translated *into*. Contrasts with **formal equivalence**.

Elohim. One of the most common biblical Hebrew words used for God (the word is a grammatically *plural* form).

ethnocentrism. "Evaluation of other cultures according to preconceptions originating in the standards and customs of one's own culture" (from Oxford Languages; https://languages.oup.com).

etymology. "The study of the origin of words and the way in which their meanings have changed throughout history" (from Oxford Languages; https://languages.oup.com).

folk etymology. An explanation of the derivation of a word that is popularly accepted and believed, although unlikely to be true from a linguistic or historical perspective. Such etymologies (which can *seem* surprisingly suitable) are often rooted in corruptions or misunderstandings of the original terms. Example: in the Bible, the name of Moses is portrayed as related to a rare Hebrew verb meaning "to draw out" (from the water); linguists point out that *-mose* was actually a common component of Egyptian names, meaning "child" or "son."

formal equivalence. Term coined by linguist Eugene Nida to refer to a style of translation marked by literal fidelity to the source text, at

Glossary

the level of word order and grammatical structure. Contrasts with **dynamic equivalence**.

Godhead. An older term used in Christian theology to refer to the concept of the Trinity (one God in three persons).

Hellenistic. Of or relating to ancient Greek history or culture.

Hexapla. An edition of the Old Testament prepared over a twenty-year period by Church father Origen sometime before 245 CE. Each of its pages (believed to number around 7,000) contained six columns that allowed comparison of the Hebrew text of the Old Testament, the Hebrew text in Greek characters, and the Greek versions of Aquila, Symmachus, the Septuagint, and Theodotion.

Johannine. Relating to the Gospel or Epistles of John in the New Testament, traditionally attributed to the Apostle John.

Kabbalah. A school of thought rooted in ancient Jewish mysticism and its related texts; from the Hebrew for "that which is received" or "the received tradition."

kairos. The right, critical, or opportune moment; from the Greek.

Little Brothers of Jesus. A Catholic male religious order inspired by the life and writings of Blessed Charles de Foucauld.

Mandatory Palestine. The region of Palestine during the period between 1923 and 1948, when it was administered by Britain under the authority of a League of Nations mandate.

minyan. The quorum of ten Jewish male adults required for certain forms of Jewish public prayer or ritual.

Mishnah. First major written collection of the Jewish interpretive traditions known as the "Oral Torah." It is also the first major work of rabbinic literature, compiled in the second century on the basis of earlier sources. Most of the Mishnah is written in Hebrew, while some parts are in Aramaic.

Nicene Creed. A profession of faith widely used in Christian liturgy, originally adopted by the First Council of Nicaea in 325 CE and subsequently expanded upon at the First Council of Constantinople in 381 CE.

Nostra aetate. The Second Vatican Council's landmark declaration on the Catholic Church's relationship to non-Christian religions, issued in October 1965.

orientalism. "The representation of Asia, especially the Middle East, in a stereotyped way that is regarded as embodying a colonialist attitude" (from Oxford Languages; https://languages.oup.com). The term was popularized by Edward Said in his 1978 book by the same title.

pagan. From the Latin for "rural," a term first used, in a derogatory sense, in the fourth century by Christians for Romans who practiced polytheism.

Pesach. Also known as Passover, an eight-day major spring festival in the Jewish religious calendar, celebrating the miraculous liberation of the Hebrew people (=Exodus) from slavery under the Egyptians.

Pesachim. A tractate of the Mishnah (and Talmud) concerned with how to properly observe *Pesach*, or Passover. See also **Mishnah**; **Pesach**; **Talmud**.

pontifex. A priest who served the Roman pantheon of gods, who mediated between common people and divinity (*pontifex* means "bridge builder" in Latin).

pontifex maximus. Title referring to the chief Roman priest (the title was sometimes vested in the Roman emperor). Subsequently adopted by the Roman Church after 1453 as one of the official titles of the pope. The abbreviation "Pont. Max." was used after the pope's name on carved inscriptions and Vatican coinage until the papacy of Benedict XVI.

Second Temple Judaism. A momentous period in Jewish history between the return from the Babylonian Exile (around 538 BCE) and the destruction of the Jerusalem Temple by the Romans in the year 70 CE. Jesus and his first followers lived toward the end of the Second Temple period.

Second Vatican Council. The largest and most representative gathering of Catholic bishops, held in Rome between 1962 and 1965, to address the relationship of the Catholic Church and its teachings to modern issues and questions in a changing world.

Septuagint. The earliest extant translation of the Hebrew Scriptures, made into Greek in the mid-third century BCE. By the time of Jesus and Paul of Tarsus, it had become the standard version of the Bible for Jews outside the Land of Israel, most of whom could no longer read Hebrew fluently.

Glossary

Sephardim. A term used to refer to Jews whose ancestors lived in Spain and Portugal (*Sepharad* in medieval Hebrew), many of whom were later forced to emigrate to North Africa, Greece, and Turkey. Often used in contrast with *Ashkenazim* (referring to Jews whose ancestors lived in Central and Eastern Europe).

Shoah. A Hebrew term, meaning "devastation" or "disaster," frequently used today as a preferred substitute for the word *Holocaust* (which was originally a biblical term referring to a category of temple sacrifice, "entirely burned up"). Many argue that *holocaust* is an inappropriate and offensive term, since it suggests something holy and good, and implies that the victims of the Nazis somehow willingly offered themselves as a sacrifice for God.

Synoptic Gospels. From the Greek for "seen together." The Gospels of Matthew, Mark, and Luke, which describe events from a similar point of view compared to that of John, are assumed to have a literary relationship to each other.

tallit/tzitzit. A traditional Jewish prayer shawl. The *tallit* is characterized by its fringes, which have religious significance for many devout Jews and are referred to as *tzitzit*.

Talmud. One of two large collections of authoritative rabbinic commentaries on Jewish law and custom (the Babylonian and Jerusalem Talmuds), built around the framework of the Mishnah, and compiled between 400 and 600 CE.

targums (or targumim). Originally spoken Aramaic translations of the Jewish Scriptures that a *meturgeman* (authorized interpreter) would give in the common language of the listeners when Hebrew was no longer commonly understood. Writing down the targum was initially prohibited; nevertheless, some targums appeared as early as the middle of the first century CE. Some targums are quite literal, whereas others are more expansive, incorporating interpretive traditions.

Third Quest for the Historical Jesus. Third phase, originating in the 1980s, of an overarching movement of academic efforts to determine what words and actions could be reliably attributed to Jesus, and to use those findings to provide portraits of the historical Jesus.

trinitarian (controversies). Referring to debates about the distinctive Christian belief in, and understanding of, God as simultaneously one-in-three. Many early Christian councils of bishops grappled with finding appropriate and adequate language to express the relationship of the three divine persons.

Vulgate. Principal Latin version of the Bible, prepared mainly by St. Jerome in the late fourth century and adopted as the standard text for the Roman Catholic Church in its liturgical life

YHWH (or the Tetragrammaton, "Four-Letter Word"). The sacred name of God in Jewish Scripture and tradition (see Exodus 3:14), which in traditional Judaism is considered so sacred that it is not pronounced aloud.

Yom Kippur. Day of Atonement; most solemn and important occasion of the Jewish religious year, an annual day of fasting, prayer, and repentance for one's sins.

Zadoc Cahn. Zadoc Cahn (1839–1905), a chief rabbi of France known for his 1899 French translation of the Hebrew Bible.

NOTES

This book draws very extensively upon André Chouraqui's three published autobiographies:

- *Ce que je crois* (Paris: B. Grasset, 1979), which was translated into English by Kenton Kilmer as *A Man in Three Worlds* (Lanham, MD: University Press of America, 1984).
- *L'amour fort comme la mort: Une autobiographie* (Love as strong as death: An autobiography) (Paris: Robert Laffont, 1990).
- *Mon testament: Le feu de l'Alliance* (My testament: The fire of the covenant) (Paris: Bayard, 2001).

Throughout these notes, references to these works will use the abbreviated titles *A Man*, *L'amour*, and *Testament*, respectively.

Any otherwise uncredited translations of non-English reference texts are my own.

Foreword

1. André Chouraqui, *A Man in Three Worlds*, trans. Kenton Kilmer (Lanham, MD: University Press of America, 1984).
2. Zalman Schachter-Shalomi viewed him as the "Nazarener Rebbe," a first-century parallel to a Hasidic tzaddik. See his essay "Jesus in Jewish-Christian-Moslem Dialogue," in *Paradigm Shift: From the Jewish Renewal Teachings of Reb Zalman Schachter-Shalomi*, ed. Ellen Singer (Northvale, NJ: Jason Aronson, Inc., 1993), 33–37.

Preface

1. The term *Shoah* ("disaster" in Hebrew) is preferred by many people today to the term *Holocaust* (from a Greek term for a sacrifice that was "completely burned up" on the altar to please a divinity).

2. Arundhati Roy, *Power Politics* (Boston: South End Press, 2001), 7.

3. A quasi-"messianic" vocation: "But now in Christ Jesus you who once were far off have been brought near by the blood of Christ" (Eph 2:13). The Italian Jewish scholar Marco Morselli speaks of a traditional Jewish understanding that "the Messiah is *ha-meqarev et ha-reḥoqim*" (he who brings near those who were far off) (Morselli, *I Passi del Messia: Per una teologia ebraica del cristianesimo* [Genoa: Marietti, 2007], 114). This probably reflects the reading of Jer 23:23 that is found in the fourth-century Jewish commentary *Mekilta de-Rabbi Ishmael*: "'I [God] am One who welcomes, not One who repels'. As it is said: 'Behold, I am a God that brings near, saith the Lord, and not a God that repels' (Jer 23:23)." (Jacob Z. Lauterbach, trans., *Mekilta de-Rabbi Ishmael*, vol. 2. [Philadelphia: Jewish Publication Society, 1949], Tractate *Amalek*, 173.) Lauterbach's footnote here explains that this interpretation relies on reading the Hebrew consonants with a particular combination of vowels.

4. *Testament*, 24, 26.

Main Text

1. A play on one of the central questions asked during the Passover Seder: "Why is this night different from all other nights?" (in Hebrew: *Mah nishtanah ha-layla ha-zeh mikol haleilot?*).

2. The title of this chapter is drawn from John Milbank's book *The Word Made Strange: Theology, Language, Culture* (Cambridge, MA: Blackwell Publishers, 1997).

3. From Rabbi Jonathan Sacks, *Not in God's Name: Confronting Religious Violence* (New York: Schocken, 2017), 227:

> Rabbi Naftali Zvi Yehudah Berlin (1817–93), head of the rabbinical seminary in Volozhin, made a fascinating comment on the biblical story of the Tower of Babel. It begins with the statement that "The whole world had one language and shared words." This, he says, was precisely what was wrong with it:
>
> "Since the views of human beings are not the same, [the builders of Babel] were concerned that no one should have a

contrary opinion. They therefore took care that no one be allowed to leave their city, and those who expressed contrary views were condemned to death by fire, as they sought to do to Abraham. Their 'shared words' became a stumbling-block because they resolved to kill anyone who did not think as they did."

Berlin sees Babel as the first totalitarian state. The "shared words" of its builders were a denial of the diversity of human opinion. Dissent was forbidden. Those who expressed it were threatened by death. Utopian-sectarian communities pride themselves on their unity, but it is secured at too high a price: hostility to those who do not share their views.

It is also worth noting that Babel, which means "gate of God," seems to be linked here with *balal*, a Hebrew word meaning "confusion."

See Northrop Frye, *The Great Code: The Bible and Literature* (London: Ark Paperbacks, 1983), 53–54.

4. Although we speak of "THE Septuagint" in English, French scholars recognize the diversity and composite nature of these versions and speak of "LES Septante" (see especially the work of Dr. Marguerite Harl and her colleagues).

5. "The Hexapla presented for comparison the Hebrew text of the Old Testament, the Hebrew text in Greek characters, and the Greek versions of Aquila, Symmachus, the Septuagint, and Theodotian in six parallel columns....In the column devoted to the Septuagint version, he indicated by the use of critical symbols the variations that occurred in Hebrew and Greek renditions. The entire work took 20 years to complete and may have filled 7,000 pages. It was available in Caesarea until about 600 and was consulted by many scholars, including Jerome in preparing for his Vulgate translation" ("Hexapla," *Encyclopaedia Britannica Online*: https://www.britannica.com/topic/Hexapla).

6. Paul V. M. Flesher and Bruce D. Chilton, *The Targums: A Critical Introduction* (Waco, TX: Baylor University Press, 2011), 27.

7. Wayne Grudem, "The Meaning of *Kephalē* ("Head"): A Response to Recent Studies," in *Recovering Biblical Manhood and*

Womanhood: A Response to Evangelical Feminism, ed. John Piper and Wayne Grudem (Wheaton, IL: Crossway Books, 2006), 445.

8. "History of the Septuagint Text," in Alfred Rahlfs's edition of the Septuagint, as cited by Grudem in "The Meaning of *Kephalē*."

9. See, e.g., Pinchas E. Lapide, *Hebrew in the Church: The Foundations of Jewish-Christian Dialogue*, trans. Erroll F. Rhodes (Grand Rapids: Eerdmans, 1984).

10. For more on this topic, see Hyam Maccoby, *Judaism on Trial: Jewish-Christian Disputations in the Middle Ages* (Rutherford, NJ: Fairleigh Dickinson University Press, 1982); Robert Chazan, *Barcelona and Beyond: The Disputation of 1263 and Its Aftermath* (Berkeley: University of California Press, 1992); Mark R. Cohen, "Interreligious Polemics," in *Under Crescent and Cross: The Jews in the Middle Ages* (Princeton, NJ: Princeton University Press, 1994), 139–61; Pinchas E. Lapide, *Hebrew in the Church: The Foundations of Jewish-Christian Dialogue* (Grand Rapids: Eerdmans, 1985); and the Hebrew texts of the Lord's Prayer/Our Father collected by Jean Carmignac, "Hebrew Translations of the Lord's Prayer: An Historical Survey," in *Biblical and Near Eastern Studies: Essays in Honor of William Sanford LaSor*, ed. Gary A. Tuttle (Grand Rapids: Eerdmans, 1978), 18–79.

11. *A Man*, 166; *L'amour*, 502, 670–72.

12. Lawrence Venuti, *The Translator's Invisibility: A History of Translation* (London: Routledge, 1995), 4–5, 20.

13. The letters *INRI*, often found above Jesus's head in images of the crucifixion, are the first letters of the Latin words *Iesus Nazarenus Rex Iudæorum* (Jesus of Nazareth, King of the Jews), representing the claim for which Jesus was crucified, according to John 19:19.

14. C. G. Montefiore, *The Synoptic Gospels*, 2nd ed. (London: Macmillan, 1927), 80.

15. Lewis Browne, *The Wisdom of Israel* (New York: Random House, 1945; Modern Library edition, 1956), 147.

16. Leora Batnizky, "Translation as Transcendence: A Glimpse into the Workshop of the Buber-Rosenzweig Bible Translation," *New German Critique* 70 (Winter 1997): 92.

17. Robert Gibbs, "The Jewish Tradition," in *A Companion to Philosophy of Religion*, ed. Philip L. Quinn and Charles Taliaferro,

Notes

Blackwell Companions to Philosophy (Cambridge, MA: Blackwell Publishers, 1999), 184.

18. Everett Fox, *The Five Books of Moses: A New Translation, with Introductions, Notes and Commentary* (New York: Schocken, 1995), x, xxii. See the review/interview by Kenneth Woodward, "In the Beginning…the Bible was written in ancient Hebrew, with nary a Thou to be had. Now comes a new vital translation that tries to capture the original flavor," *Newsweek*, Jan. 15, 1996.

19. Fox, *Five Books of Moses*, 36.

20. John Meier, "The Present State of the 'Third Quest' for the Historical Jesus: Loss and Gain," *Biblica* 80, no. 4 (1999): 459–87, quoting 486.

21. See also Erasmo Leiva-Merikakis, *Fire of Mercy, Heart of the Word: Meditations on the Gospel According to Saint Matthew*, 2 vols. (San Francisco: Ignatius Press, 1996).

22. André Chouraqui, "Le substrat sémitique du Nouveau Testament," *L'Univers de la Bible*, vol. 8, 11, 12; Chouraqui, "Liminaire pour un Pacte Neuf": https://nachouraqui.tripod.com/id90.htm.

23. Joseph Sarachek, in his *The Doctrine of the Messiah in Medieval Jewish Literature* (Harmon Press, 1932), 112, cites as his source vol. 1 of D. Kahana's edition of Ibn Ezra's collected poetic works (Warsaw, 1922), 166. The translation used here is from Dr. Avigail Rock's lecture on ibn Ezra (https://www.etzion.org.il/en/lecture-13-r-avraham-ibn-ezra-part-i; fn. 24); several authors mention this palindrome, but without providing an exact reference for it.

24. Northrop Frye, *The Great Code: The Bible and Literature* (Toronto: University of Toronto Press, 2006), 71. In Hebrew, "from these stones" would be מִן־הָאֲבָנִים הָאֵלֶּה and "children" would be בָּנִים. Note the Hebrew consonants, which are identical.

25. Frye, *The Great Code*, 53–54; John F. A. Sawyer, *Sacred Languages and Sacred Texts* (London: Routledge, 1999), 115. See also Maurice Casey, *Aramaic Sources of Mark's Gospel*, Society for New Testament Studies Monograph Series volume 102 (Cambridge: Cambridge University Press, 1999), 30; Joachim Jeremias, *The Eucharistic Words of Jesus* (New York: Scribner, 1966), 56, 231; Claude Tresmontant, *The Hebrew Christ: Language in the Age of the Gospels* (Chicago: Franciscan Herald Press, 1989), 64, 146, 230.

26. Jože Krašovec, *The Transformation of Biblical Proper Names* (London: T & T Clark, 2019), 4.

27. On this suggestion, see Mikeal C. Parsons, *Luke*, Paideia Commentary series (Grand Rapids: Baker Academic, 2015): "Jesus announces: 'Today, salvation has come to this house.' Jesus' name, Yeshua, means 'salvation,' and in one sense, salvation has come to this house, in the very person of Jesus." (n.p.).

28. Some patristic sources speak of a Hebrew-language version of Matthew's Gospel in particular: "There seems to be evidence for multiple Semitic Gospels under various titles, sometimes associated with Matthew, but Jerome apparently knows of only one such Gospel.... Jerome mentions this 'Hebrew' Gospel several times...and says that he translated it into Greek and Latin." (Edmon L. Gallagher, *Hebrew Scripture in Patristic Biblical Theory: Canon, Language, Text* [Leiden: Brill, 2012], 127n78).

29. The names of the Virgin Mary's parents, according to Catholic tradition, rooted in the apocryphal second-century *Protevangelium [Infancy Gospel] of James*. See "Protevangelium of James," in *New Testament Apocrypha*, vol. 1: *Gospels and Other Writings*, ed. Wilhelm Schneemelcher, trans. R. McL. Wilson (Louisville, KY: Westminster John Knox Press, 2003), 421–39.

30. Franz Zorell, "Maria, soror Mosis et Maria, Mater Dei," *Verbum Domini 6* (1926), 257–63.

31. Luis Díez Merino, "María, hermana de Moisés, en la tradición targúmica," (Santuario de Torreciudad: Scripta de Maria, 1984): https://studylib.es/doc/8149061/mar%C3%ADa--hermana-de-mois%C3%A9s--en-la-tradici%C3%B3n-targ%C3%BAmica.

32. Jean Carmignac, *The Birth of the Synoptics*, as cited in Karl Keating, *What Catholics Really Believe: Answers to Common Misconceptions about the Faith* (San Francisco: Ignatius Press, 2010), 103. See also René Laurentin, "Traces d'allusions étymologiques en Luc 1–2," *Biblica* 37 (1956): 435–56 and 38 (1957): 1–23.

33. Jean-Pierre Isbouts, *Young Jesus: Restoring the "Lost Years" of a Social Activist and Religious Dissident* (New York: Sterling Publishing, 2008), 22.

34. Isbouts, *Young Jesus*, 23.

Notes

35. R. T. France, *The Gospel of Mark: A Commentary on the Greek Text*, New International Greek Testament Commentary (Grand Rapids: Eerdmans, 2002), 34.

36. *Pesaḥim* is the third tractate in *Moed*, an order of the Mishnah concerned with the correct observance of festivals (in the case of *Pesaḥim*, specifically the observance of *Pesaḥ* or Passover).

37. In Psalm 121:4, God is spoken of as the *Shomer Yisrael* (the one who watches over and protects his people, Israel).

38. St. Augustine, *Sermons III/4 (94A to 174A)*, The Works of St. Augustine, trans. Edmund Hill (Brooklyn: New City Press, 1992), 319. As the translator comments, "The name probably, in fact, meant fortress or castle, like such European place names as Newcastle, or Castilla" (323).

39. A different passage, Zechariah 6:11–13, speaks of "a man whose name is The Branch," a mysterious royal figure who will build God's Temple in the future. Although the Hebrew word used there (*tzamah*) is different from the *netzer* of Isaiah, by the time of Jesus, the two terms were apparently being used interchangeably, as a reference to the awaited Messiah. (See Mary L. Coloe, "John's Portrait of Jesus," in *The Blackwell Companion to Jesus*, ed. Delbert Burkett [Oxford: Wiley Blackwell, 2004], 75).

40. Richard R. Losch, *The Uttermost Part of the Earth: A Guide to Places in the Bible* (Grand Rapids: Eerdmans, 2005), 51.

41. For further detail on the origins of these place names, see these sources: on Beersheba, Ronald L. Eisenberg, *Dictionary of Jewish Terms: A Guide to the Language of Judaism* (Rockville, MN: Schreiber Publications, 2011), 42; on Bethlehem, Richard R. Losch, *The Uttermost Part of the Earth: A Guide to Places in the Bible* (Grand Rapids: Eerdmans, 2005), 51; on Magdala, John J. Rousseau, *Jesus and His World: An Archaeological and Cultural Dictionary* (London: SCM Press, 1996), 189; on Nazareth, Bargil Pixner, *With Jesus through Galilee According to the Fifth Gospel* (Rosh Pina, Israel: Corazin Publishing, 1992), 14–15; and on Samaria, *The Works of St. Augustine*, trans. Edmund Hill, vol. ? (Brooklyn: New City Press, 1992), 323n14.

42. From the Hebrew translation of the New Testament made by Franz Delitzsch and published in Berlin in 1901.

43. Jean-François Féraud, *Dictionnaire critique de la langue française* (Marseille: Mossy, 1787–88), A750a; available online at the ARTFL Project: https://artfl-project.uchicago.edu/content/dictionnaires-dautrefois.

44. Herman N. Ridderbos, *The Gospel According to John: A Theological Commentary* (Grand Rapids: Ecrdmans, 1997), 637.

45. For instance: Bruce D. Chilton, *Rabbi Jesus: An Intimate Biography* (New York: Doubleday, 2000); William E. Phipps, *The Wisdom and Wit of Rabbi Jesus* (Louisville, KY: Westminster John Knox Press, 1993); Matthew Hoffman, *From Rebel to Rabbi: Reclaiming Jesus and the Making of Modern Jewish Culture* (Palo Alto, CA: Stanford University Press, 2007); Frauke Büchner, *Rabbi Jesus und die Anfänge einer christlichen Lernkultur. Zeitschrift für Pädagogik und Theologie*, Jg 53, 2 (Frankfurt am Main: Diesterweg, 2001); Susannah Heschel, "From Rabbi to Aryan: The Political Use of Jesus in Jewish-Christian Dialogue" (video lecture); Christopher F. Mooney Lecture in Theology, Religion and Society, Fairfield University, Nov. 7, 2002; Bernard Chouraqui, *Jésus, le rabbi de Nazareth* (Paris: La Différence, 1990); Jacques Baldet, *Histoire de Rabbi Jésus* (Paris: Imago, 2003); Jacquot Grunewald, *Chalom, Jésus! Lettre d'un rabbin d'aujourd'hui au rabbi de Nazareth* (Paris: Albin Michel Spiritualités, 2000).

46. See Louis Jacobs, "Sherira Gaon," in *The Jewish Religion: A Companion* (Oxford: Oxford University Press, 1995), 463.

47. See, for instance, Catherine Hezser, "The Lack of Rabbinic Evidence for a Pre-70 Usage of the Title 'Rabbi,'" in *The Social Structure of the Rabbinic Movement in Roman Palestine*, Texte und Studien zum antiken Judentum 66 (Tübingen: Mohr Siebeck, 1997), 63–64, and particularly the notes on page 58 of David E. Garland, *The Intention of Matthew 23*, Supplements to *Novum Testamentum* 52 (Leiden: Brill, 1979).

48. Shaye J. D. Cohen, "Epigraphical Rabbis," in *Jewish Quarterly Review*, new series, 72, no. 1 (July 1981): 9, 16, 17.

49. Bruce Chilton, "Mapping a Place for Jesus," in *The Missing Jesus: Rabbinic Judaism and the New Testament*, ed. Bruce Chilton, Craig A. Evans, and Jacob Neusner (Boston: Brill Academic Publishers, 2002), 42–43. My emphasis.

50. Elias Hutter (1553–1605) was a German biblical scholar, who translated the New Testament into Hebrew as part of his 1599 polyglot

Notes

Bible, which included parallel translations in 12 languages. Franz Delitzsch (1813–90) was a German Lutheran pastor and biblical scholar with a particular zeal for missionary efforts among Jews. In 1877, he produced a translation of the New Testament into Hebrew, which remains in print today. Isaac Salkinson (1820–83) was born into an Orthodox Jewish family in Lithuania. He converted to Christianity in 1849, and later became a Presbyterian minister and translator into Hebrew. His Hebrew translation of the New Testament (incomplete at the time of his death) was completed by his good friend (and fellow convert) David Ginsburg (1831–1914) and published in 1885. It also remains in print today.

51. *L'Univers de la Bible*, vol. 8, 38.

52. A. S. van der Woude and Theodoor Christiaan Vriezen, *Ancient Israelite and Early Jewish Literature* (Leiden: Brill, 2005), 308.

53. Charlton T. Lewis and Charles Short, *A Latin Dictionary* (Oxford: Clarendon Press, 1879).

54. "*Manthanō*," in *A Greek-English Lexicon of the New Testament Based on Semantic Domains*, ed. J. P. Louw and E. A. Nida, 2nd ed. (New York: United Bible Societies, 1988).

55. Everett Ferguson, *Backgrounds of Early Christianity*, 2nd ed. (Grand Rapids: Eerdmans, 1993), 3, 252.

56. Norman Perrin and Dennis C. Duling, *The New Testament, An Introduction: Proclamation and Parenesis, Myth and History* (San Diego, CA: Harcourt Brace Jovanovich, 1982), 12.

57. Thomas F. Torrance, *Atonement: The Person and Work of Christ* (London: InterVarsity Press, 2014), 317.

58. TOB = Traduction œcuménique de la Bible (Ecumenical Translation of the Bible)

BFC = Bible en français courant (The Bible in Contemporary French)

B_DEJ = Bible de Jérusalem (The French edition of the Jerusalem Bible)

B_AY = La Bible: Nouvelle traduction (The Bible: A New Translation, published by the Bayard Press)

Maredsous = The Bible as translated by the monks of Maredsous, Belgium

59. See, e.g., the discussion in Julie H. Danan, "The Divine Voice in Scripture: Ruah ha-Kodesh in Rabbinic Literature" (PhD diss., University of Texas at Austin, 2009).

60. On this topic, see Richard Killough, "A Reexamination of the Concept of Spirit in Christian Theology," *American Journal of Theology & Philosophy* 6 (1985): 2–3, 141; Michael E. Lodahl, *Shekhinah/Spirit: Divine Presence in Jewish and Christian Traditions* (Eugene, OR: Wipf & Stock, 2012), 45–46; Alasdair Heron, *The Holy Spirit* (Philadelphia: Westminster Press, 1983), 8.

61. John Gill, *Expositions on the Old and New Testaments*, 3 vols., 1746–48 (Ada, MI: Baker Books, 1982). Gill's commentary is also available online: https://www.studylight.org/commentaries/eng/geb.html.

62. Paula Fredriksen, *Jesus of Nazareth, King of the Jews: A Jewish Life and the Emergence of Christianity* (New York: Knopf, 1999), 109.

63. Shaye J.D. Cohen, *The Beginnings of Jewishness: Boundaries, Varieties, Uncertainties*, Hellenistic Culture and Society 31 (Berkeley: University of California Press, 1999), 33.

64. Amy-Jill Levine, *The Misunderstood Jew: The Church and the Scandal of the Jewish Jesus* (San Francisco: HarperSanFrancisco, 2006), 23–24.

65. For example, David Buttrick in *Speaking Jesus: Homiletic Theology and the Sermon on the Mount* (Louisville, KY: Westminster John Knox Press, 2002), 65.

66. It is worth noting that the original, 1976 edition of Chouraqui's New Testament has, instead, *allégresses* (happinesses).

67. André Chouraqui, *Un pacte neuf* (Turnhout, Belgium: Brépols, 1984). Note to Matthew 5:6.

68. Erasmo Leiva-Merikakis, *Fire of Mercy, Heart of the Word: Meditations on the Gospel According to Saint Matthew*, vol. 1 (San Francisco: Ignatius Press, 1996), 185.

69. Jean-Marie de Bourqueney, "La théologie du *Process* ou la rénovation du langage théologique," in *Manifeste pour un christianisme d'avenir*, ed. Robert Ageneau, Serge Couderc, Robert Dumont and Jacques Musset (Paris: Éditions Karthala, 2020), 67.

70. "Flowers," in *Dictionary of Biblical Imagery*, ed. Leland Ryken, James C. Wilhoit, and Tremper Longman III (Downers Grove, IL: InterVarsity Press, 1998), 294.

Notes

71. Léopold Sabourin, *Il Vangelo di Matteo: Teologia e exegesi*, Nuova edizione aumentata, vol. 1 ([Rome?]: Edizioni Paolini, 1976), 462.

72. Eugène Levesque, "Lis," in *Dictionnaire de la Bible*, ed. F. Vigouroux (Paris: Letouzey et Ané, 1912), vol. 4, col. 283.

73. English translation from the Latin original by Sister Wilfrid Parsons, *St. Augustine: Letters*, vol. 1. [1–82] (New York: Fathers of the Church, 1951), 327.

74. For this reason, the French biblical resource site Bibliorama counsels: "Before diving into the Chouraqui Bible, it is preferable to have at least some basic background in Hebrew; otherwise, you risk being destabilized [thrown off balance] by reading it"; https://www.bibliorama.org/bible/la-bible-chouraqui/.

75. On this, see Máire Byrne, *The Names of God in Judaism, Christianity and Islam: A Basis for Interfaith Dialogue* (London: Bloomsbury, 2011), 27–28.

76. "Stressing the word שחוברה, R. Johanan adduces from the verse that Jerusalem has a חברה, a companion (or prototype) in heaven. Both are said to be situated exactly opposite each other. [The verse in Hosea is thus taken to mean: There is a holy (city) in thy midst (referring to the earthly Jerusalem) and I (i.e., God) will not enter the city (the heavenly Jerusalem)]." (Soncino Talmud, b. *Ta'anit* 5a and accompanying notes).

77. On this, also see Samuel A. Berman, *Midrash Tanhuma-Yelammedenu: An English Translation of Genesis and Exodus from the Printed Version of Tanhuma-Yelammedenu with an Introduction, Notes and Indexes* (Hoboken, NJ: Ktav, 1995); and Daniel Chanan Matt, *The Zohar* (Stanford, CA: Stanford University Press, 2003).

78. In the original, 1976 edition, Chouraqui has simply "is joyful." It seems that Chouraqui is attempting to draw a linguistic and semantic link between the Greek verb *chairein* (to rejoice) and the French verb *chérir* (to cherish) on the basis of the cluster of consonants they have in common (*ch-r*), but it is not clear that there is a connection between the two. The Greek noun *charis*—which is cognate to *chairein*—certainly *can* have the meaning of "loving-kindness" or "favorable disposition toward," but it is questionable whether it rises to the level of "cherishing." However, Jean Girod, a French professor of philosophy in the early twentieth century, also made this association; he speaks of the

Christian understanding of charity, "so well captured in its name, taken from the Greek *chairein*, 'to love' or 'to cherish.'" (*Démocratie, patrie et humanité* [Paris: Félix Alcan, 1908], 73). This seems, however, to be a fairly marginal interpretation, and is perhaps an example of a case where Chouraqui's etymological excavations may have led him to conclusions that, while intriguing, seem forced or fanciful at best.

79. This unique graphic logogram (Y$_{\text{H}}^{\text{ADONAI}}$$_{\text{W}}^{\text{H}}$H) that Chouraqui uses throughout his translations to indicate the four-letter sacred name of God (יהוה; YHWH, perhaps "Yahweh," and often mistakenly rendered as "Jehovah" in older translations), reminds us of the ancient Jewish tradition that God's personal name was something so utterly sacred and transcendent that it should not be spoken out loud (to avoid disrespect). As a result, Hebrew Biblical manuscripts came to incorporate signs in the text, which told the reader that the word *Adonai* (Lord, or "my Lord") should be substituted in public proclamation wherever YHWH occurred in the text. In the Masoretic scribal tradition, this often included pairing the *consonants* of YHWH with the *vowels* of Adonai. Several of the classical Hebrew types designed by Sami Artur Mandelbaum of Samtype (https:// www .myfonts .com/ foundry/ samtype/) incorporate a similar graphic convention:): אֲדֹנָי

This reticence in pronouncing the Name remains the practice for most Jews today (and for many Christians, as was highlighted by the Vatican in a 2008 letter to the world's Catholic bishops on this topic: https://www.usccb.org/prayer-and-worship/the-mass/frequently-asked-questions/upload/name-of-god.pdf).

80. "Theodor Herzl: Audience with Pope Pius X (1904)," Primary Texts on History of Relations, Council of Centers on Jewish-Christian Relations, https://www.ccjr.us/dialogika-resources/primary-texts-from-the-history-of-the-relationship/herzl1904.

81. On this history, see especially Menahem R. Macina, "L'Église à l'épreuve des Juifs: L'abolition d'*Amici Israel* (1926–1928)": https://www.academia.edu/8753439/L%C3%89glise_%C3%A0_l%C3%A9preuve_des_Juifs_Labolition_dAmici_Israel_1926_1928_.

82. Cyril Aslanov, *Pour comprendre la Bible: La leçon d'André Chouraqui* (Paris: Éditions du Rocher, 1999), 12.

Notes

83. Francine Kaufmann, "Traduire la Bible et le Coran à Jérusalem: André Chouraqui," *Meta: Journal des traducteurs* 43, no. 1 (March 1998), 144: http://www.erudit.org/revue/meta/1998/v43/n1/003294ar.html.

84. *Testament*, 24–25.
85. *L'amour*, 54.
86. *L'amour*, 62.
87. *A Man*, 70.
88. *L'amour*, 93.
89. *L'amour*, 72–73.
90. *L'amour*, 74, 81.
91. *L'amour*, 101–2.
92. Perhaps the authors of his Arabic textbooks?
93. *L'amour*, 122.
94. *A Man*, 76.
95. Chouraqui is perhaps alluding here to a famous collection of accounts from the First Crusade by this title, compiled by the Benedictine abbot Guibert of Nogent (died ca. 1124), first printed in Latin in the early 1600s, and translated into French in 1825.
96. *L'amour*, 108–9.
97. *L'amour*, 128.
98. *A Man*, 81, 84–85.
99. *A Man*, 88.
100. *A Man*, 75.
101. *L'amour*, 213, 214, 215.
102. One historian describes their first, eventful encounter this way: "On November 11, 1939, with the Germans threatening to invade France, Boyer on foot collided by a bicycle ridden by a Jewish law student named André Chouraqui" (Robert O. Gjerdingen, "A Sickly Young Woman Speaks Elegant Harmony," chapter 17 in *Child Composers in the Old Conservatories: How Orphans Became Elite Musicians* [New York: Oxford University Press, 2020], 235).
103. *L'amour*, 293.
104. *L'amour*, 308.
105. *L'amour*, 318.
106. *L'amour*, 321.
107. It seems that Colette was also involved in these efforts, to the degree her health permitted: "In solidarity she converted to Judaism and

followed him into the Resistance in central France, where the guerrilla fighters were called the Maquis. Although confined to a sanatorium because of her health for part of the war, when able she served as a courier for the Maquis." (Gjerdingen, "A Sickly Young Woman," 235).

108. Herbert R. Lottman, *Albert Camus: A Biography* (Garden City, NY: Doubleday, 1979), 259.

109. Patrick Henry, "Albert Camus, Panelier and *La Peste*," in *Literary Imagination: The Review of the Association of Literary Scholars and Critics*, 5, no. 3 (2003), 383–404: http://litimag.oxfordjournals.org/cgi/reprint/5/3/383.pdf.

110. Patrick Henry, *We Only Know Men: The Rescue of Jews in France during the Holocaust* (Washington, DC: Catholic University of America Press, 2007), 130.

111. *L'amour*, 329–30.

112. *A Man*, 110–11.

113. *A Man*, 118.

114. André Chouraqui, "Hommage à Jules Isaac: Conférence d'André Chouraqui" (Amitié judéo-chrétienne de Marseille, December 17, 1963): http://judaisme.sdv.fr/perso/jisaac/chouraq.htm.

115. André Chouraqui, *Accepter l'Autre en sa différence* (Paris: Desclée de Brouwer, 2013), 113–14.

116. André Chouraqui, *Le destin d'Israël: Correspondances avec Jules Isaac, Jacques Ellul, Jacques Maritain et Marc Chagall; Entretiens avec Paul Claudel* (Paris: Éditions Parole et Silence, 2007), 24.

117. Chouraqui, "Hommage à Jules Isaac."

118. *L'amour*, 366.

119. *L'amour*, 369.

120. *L'amour*, 371.

121. *L'amour*, 418–19.

122. *L'amour*, 421.

123. *L'amour*, 422.

124. *L'amour*, 423.

125. *L'amour*, 422.

126. *L'amour*, 447.

127. *L'amour*, 437.

128. *L'amour*, 439.

129. *L'amour*, 441–42.

Notes

130. *L'amour*, 464. The text here is somewhat ambiguous. Pope John XXIII had actually died in June 1963, to be succeeded by Pope Paul VI, under whose leadership *Nostra aetate* was voted on and eventually promulgated. It is possible that Chouraqui is referring here to his *earlier* meetings with John XXIII (i.e., before the pope's death); if Chouraqui is suggesting that he met John XXIII in September 1965, his memory is mistaken, or he has accidentally substituted the earlier pope's name for the latter's.

131. *L'amour*, 468.
132. *L'amour*, 483.
133. *L'amour*, 486–87.
134. *L'amour*, 490–91.
135. *L'amour*, 485.
136. *L'amour*, 498.
137. *L'amour*, 502.
138. http://www.andrechouraqui.com/actu/temoin1.htm.
139. https://www.thetimes.co.uk/article/andre-chouraqui-t0j8wl3fccm.
140. Henri Tincq, "Nécrologie: André Chouraqui, traducteur et homme politique." *Le Monde* (July 11, 2007): https://www.lemonde.fr/disparitions/article/2007/07/11/andre-chouraqui-traducteur-et-homme-politique_934280_3382.html.
141. https://dafina.net/forums/read.php?48,175885,176557.
142. Patricia Briel, "Une vie au service de la paix religieuse," *Le Temps* (July 10, 2007): https://www.letemps.ch/societe/une-vie-service-paix-religieuse.
143. "Oraison funèbre pour André Chouraqui," https://andrechouraqui.com/andre-chouraqui/en-souvenir-dandre-chouraqui-2/.
144. Bluma Finkelstein, *L'écrivain juif et les Évangiles* (Paris: Éditions Beauchesne, 1991), 10.
145. George W. Bush, "'Islam Is Peace,' Says President," The White House, September 17, 2001, https://georgewbush-whitehouse.archives.gov/news/releases/2001/09/20010917-11.html.
146. *Testament*, 27.

BIBLIOGRAPHY

Almogi, Yosef. *Total Commitment*. East Brunswick, NJ: Cornwall, 1982.
Aslanov, Cyril. *Pour comprendre la Bible: La leçon d'André Chouraqui*. Paris: du Rocher, 1999.
Augustine. *The Works of St. Augustine*. Translated by Edmund Hill. Brooklyn: New City Press, 1992.
Aveline, Jean-Marc, ed. *Humanismes et religions: Albert Camus et Paul Ricœur*. Münster: LIT Verlag, 2014.
Baldet, Jacques. *Histoire de Rabbi Jésus*. Paris: Imago, 2003.
Batnizky, Leora. "Translation as Transcendence: A Glimpse into the Workshop of the Buber-Rosenzweig Bible Translation." *New German Critique* 70 (Winter 1997).
Ben-Gurion, David. *Ben-Gurion Looks at the Bible*. Translated by Jonathan Kolatch. Middle Village, NY: Jonathan David Publishers, 1972.
Ben-Ur, Aviva. *Sephardic Jews in America: A Diasporic History*. New York: New York University Press, 2009.
Berman, Samuel A. *Midrash Tanhuma-Yelammedenu: An English Translation of Genesis and Exodus from the Printed Version of Tanhuma-Yelammedenu with an Introduction, Notes and Indexes*. Hoboken, NJ: Ktav, 1995.
Buby, Bertrand. *Mary of Galilee*. Vol. 2, *Woman of Israel—Daughter of Zion*. New York: Alba House, 1995.
Büchner, Frauke. *Rabbi Jesus und die Anfänge einer christlichen Lernkultur*. Zeitschrift für Pädagogik und Theologie, Jg 53. Frankfurt am Main: Diesterweg, 2001.
Byrne, Máire. *The Names of God in Judaism, Christianity and Islam: A Basis for Interfaith Dialogue*. London: Bloomsbury, 2011.
Chazan, Robert. *Barcelona and Beyond: The Disputation of 1263 and Its Aftermath*. Berkeley: University of California Press, 1992.
Chilton, Bruce D. *Rabbi Jesus: An Intimate Biography*. New York: Doubleday, 2000.

Chilton, Bruce D., et. al., eds. *The Missing Jesus: Rabbinic Judaism and the New Testament*. Leiden: Brill, 2002.

Chouraqui, André. *Accepter l'autre en sa différence*. Paris: Desclée de Brouwer, 2013.

———. *L'amour fort comme la mort*. Paris: Éditions Robert Laffont, 1990.

———. *Ce que je crois*. Paris: B. Grasset, 1979.

———. *Chroniques de Baba: Lettres d'Abraham Meyer, mon grand-père, à ses fils 1914–1918*. Paris: Éditions Bibliophane, 1998.

———. *La Condition juridique de l'Israélite marocain*. Paris: Presses du livre français, 1950.

———. *Le Coran: L'Appel*. Paris: Robert Laffont, 1990.

———. "Création de l'État d'Israël." PhD diss, Université de Paris, 1948.

———. *Le destin d'Israël: Correspondances avec Jules Isaac, Jacques Ellul, Jacques Maritain et Marc Chagall; Entretiens avec Paul Claudel*. Paris: Éditions Parole et Silence, 2007.

———. "Hommage à Jules Isaac." Lecture to the Amitié judéo-chrétienne de Marseille, December 17, 1963. http://judaisme.sdv.fr/perso/jisaac/chouraq.htm.

———. "Jules Isaac, Une vie et œuvre de combat." *Cahiers de l'Association des amis de Jules Isaac*, no. 3.

———. *Lettre à un ami arabe*. Paris: Mame, 1969.

———. *Lettre à un ami chrétien*. Paris: Fayard, 1971.

———. *Mon testament: Le feu de l'Alliance*. Paris: Bayard, 2001.

———. *Les Psaumes: Louanges*. Paris: Presses universitaires de France, 1955.

———. *La reconnaissance: Le Saint-Siège, les Juifs et Israël*. Paris: Robert Laffont, 1992.

———. *Retour aux racines: Entretiens avec Jacques Deschanel*. Paris: Le Centurion, 1981.

———. *Vivre pour Jérusalem*. Paris: Desclée de Brouwer, 1973.

Translations:

———. *Between East and West: A History of the Jews of North Africa*. Translated by Michael M. Bernet. Philadelphia, 1968.

Bibliography

———, translated by Kenton Kilmer. *A Man in Three Worlds*. Lanham, MD: University Press of America, 1984.

Chouraqui, André, and Colette Boyer. *Ton étoile et ta croix*. Paris. Éditions du Rocher, 1998.

Chouraqui, André, and Jean Daniélou. *Verse et controverse: Les Juifs*. Paris: Éditions Beauchesne, 1966.

Chouraqui, Bernard. *Jésus, le rabbi de Nazareth*. Paris: La Différence, 1990.

Cohen, Mark R. *Under Crescent and Cross: The Jews in the Middle Ages*. Princeton, NJ: Princeton University Press, 1994.

Cohen, Shaye J. D. *The Beginnings of Jewishness: Boundaries, Varieties, Uncertainties*. Hellenistic Culture and Society 31. Berkeley: University of California Press, 1999.

———. "Epigraphical Rabbis." *JQR*, new series, 72 (July 1981).

Culpepper, R. Alan. *John, the Son of Zebedee: The Life of a Legend*. Studies on Personalities of the New Testament. Columbia: University of South Carolina Press, 1994.

Danan, Julie H. "The Divine Voice in Scripture: Ruah ha-Kodesh in Rabbinic Literature." PhD diss., University of Texas at Austin, 2009.

Dendane, Sid Ahmed. *L'Algérie vue de l'intérieur: Étude historique et sociologique*. Paris: Publibook, 2007.

Díez Merino, I. "Maria, hermana de Moises, en la tradición targúmica." Santuario de Torreciudad: Scripta de Maria, 1984.

Eisenberg, Ronald L. *Dictionary of Jewish Terms: A Guide to the Language of Judaism*. Rockville, MN: Schreiber Publications, 2011.

———. *The 613 Mitzvot: A Contemporary Guide to the Commandments of Judaism*. Rockville, MD: Schreiber, 2005.

Féraud, Jean-François. *Dictionnaire critique de la langue française*. Marseille: Mossy, 1787.

Ferguson, Everett. *Backgrounds of Early Christianity*. 2nd ed. Grand Rapids: Eerdmans, 1993.

Finkelstein, Bluma. *L'écrivain juif et les Évangiles*. Paris: Beauchesne, 1991.

Flesher, Paul V. M., and Bruce D. Chilton. *The Targums: A Critical Introduction*. Waco, TX: Baylor University Press, 2011.

Fontenrose, Joseph. *The Delphic Oracle, Its Responses and Operations with a Catalogue of Responses*. Berkeley: University of California Press, 1978.

Fredriksen, Paula. *Jesus of Nazareth, King of the Jews: A Jewish Life and the Emergence of Christianity*. New York: Knopf, 1999.

Frieman, Shulamis. *Who's Who in the Talmud*. Northvale, NJ: Jason Aronson, 1995.

Frye, Northrop. *The Great Code: The Bible and Literature*. London: Ark Paperbacks, 1983.

Garland, David E. *The Intention of Matthew 23*. Supplements to Novum Testamentum 52. Leiden: Brill, 1979.

Gilbert, Arthur. *The Vatican Council and the Jews*. Cleveland: World Publishing, 1968.

Gómez-Rivas, Camilo. *Law and the Islamization of Morocco under the Almoravids*. Leiden: Brill, 2014.

Grunewald, Jacquot. *Chalom, Jésus! Lettre d'un rabbin d'aujourd'hui au rabbi de Nazareth*. Paris: Albin Michel Spiritualités, 2000.

Henry, Patrick. "Albert Camus, Panelier and La Peste." *Literary Imagination: The Review of the Association of Literary Scholars and Critics*, 5, no. 3 (2003).

Heron, Alasdair. *The Holy Spirit*. Philadelphia: Westminster Press, 1983.

Heschel, Susannah. "From Rabbi to Aryan: The Political Use of Jesus in Jewish-Christian Dialogue" [video lecture]. Christopher F. Mooney, SJ, Lecture in Theology, Religion and Society, Fairfield University, Nov. 7, 2002.

Hezser, Catherine. *The Social Structure of the Rabbinic Movement in Roman Palestine*. Texte und Studien zum antiken Judentum 66. Tübingen: Mohr Siebeck, 1997.

Hoffman, Matthew. *From Rebel to Rabbi: Reclaiming Jesus and the Making of Modern Jewish Culture*. Palo Alto, CA: Stanford University Press, 2007.

Jacobs, Louis. *The Jewish Religion: A Companion*. Oxford: Oxford University Press, 1995.

Jones, G. Lloyd. *The Discovery of Hebrew in Tudor England: A Third Language*. Manchester: Manchester University Press, 1983.

Bibliography

Kaufmann, Francine. "Au confluent de trois continents—André Chouraqui." *Ariel: Revue israélienne des arts et des lettres* 105 (March 1998).

———. "Traduire la Bible et le Coran à Jérusalem: André Chouraqui." *Meta: Journal des traducteurs* 43, no. 1.

Keating, Karl. *What Catholics Really Believe: Answers to Common Misconceptions about the Faith*. San Francisco: Ignatius Press, 2010.

Killough, Karl. "A Reexamination of the Concept of Spirit in Christian Theology." *American Journal of Theology & Philosophy* 6.

Krašovec, Jože. *The Transformation of Biblical Proper Names*. Edinburgh: T&T Clark, 2010.

Küng, Hans. *My Struggle for Freedom: A Memoir*. London: Continuum, 2004.

Lapide, Pinchas E. *Hebrew in the Church: The Foundations of Jewish-Christian Dialogue*. Grand Rapids: Eerdmans, 1985.

Leiva-Merikakis, Erasmo. *Fire of Mercy, Heart of the Word: Meditations on the Gospel According to Saint Matthew*. San Francisco: Ignatius Press, 2013.

Levine, Amy-Jill. *The Misunderstood Jew: The Church and the Scandal of the Jewish Jesus*. San Francisco: HarperSanFrancisco, 2006.

Lewis, Charlton T., and Charles Short. *A Latin Dictionary*. Oxford: Clarendon Press, 1879.

Lodahl, Michael E. *Shekhinah/Spirit: Divine Presence in Jewish and Christian Traditions*. Eugene, OR: Wipf & Stock, 2012.

Long, Lynne. *Translation and Religion: Holy Untranslatable?* Topics in Translation 28. Clevedon, UK: Multilingual Matters, 2005.

Losch, Richard R. *The Uttermost Part of the Earth: A Guide to Places in the Bible*. Grand Rapids: Eerdmans, 2005.

Louw, J. P., and E. A. Nida, eds. *A Greek-English Lexicon of the New Testament Based on Semantic Domains*. 2nd ed. New York: United Bible Societies, 1988.

Maccoby, Hyam. *Judaism on Trial: Jewish-Christian Disputations in the Middle Ages*. Rutherford, NJ: Fairleigh Dickinson University Press, 1982.

Matt, Daniel Chanan. *The Zohar*. Stanford, CA: Stanford University Press, 2003.

Meier, John. "The Present State of the 'Third Quest' for the Historical Jesus: Loss and Gain." *Biblica* 80, no. 4 (1999).

Merkle, John C., and Walter J. Harrelson, eds. *Faith Transformed: Christian Encounters with Jews and Judaism.* Collegeville, MN: Liturgical Press, 2003.

Miller, John H., ed. *Vatican II: An Inter-faith Appraisal.* Notre Dame, IN: University of Notre Dame Press, 1966.

Montefiore, C. G. *The Synoptic Gospels.* 2nd ed. London: Macmillan, 1927.

Morselli, Marco. *I passi del Messia: Per una teologia ebraica del cristianesimo.* Genoa: Marietti, 2007.

Neusner, Jacob. *Life of Rabban Yohanan Ben Zakkai, ca. 1-80 C.E.* Leiden: Brill, 1962.

ibn Paqûda, Bahya. *André Chouraqui présente et traduit Bachya Ibn Paqûda, Les Devoirs des Cœurs.* 5th ed. Translated by André Chouraqui. Paris: Bibliophane/Daniel Radford, 2002.

Parsons, Wilfrid. *St. Augustine: Letters.* Vol. 1. New York: Fathers of the Church, 1951.

Perrin, Norman, and Dennis C. Duling. *The New Testament, An Introduction: Proclamation and Parenesis, Myth and History.* San Diego: Harcourt Brace Jovanovich, 1982.

Phipps, William E. *The Wisdom and Wit of Rabbi Jesus.* Louisville, KY: Westminster John Knox Press, 1993.

Pixner, Bargil. *With Jesus through Galilee According to the Fifth Gospel.* Rosh Pina, Israel: Corazin Publishing, 1992.

Poznanski, Renée. *Jews in France during World War II.* The Tauber Institute for the Study of European Jewry series. Hanover: Brandeis University Press, in association with the United States Holocaust Memorial Museum, 2001.

Quinn, Philip L., and Charles Taliaferro, eds. *A Companion to Philosophy of Religion.* Blackwell Companions to Philosophy. Cambridge, MA: Blackwell Publishers, 1999.

Ridderbos, Herman N. *The Gospel According to John: A Theological Commentary.* Grand Rapids: Eerdmans, 1997.

Rousseau, John J. *Jesus and His World: An Archaeological and Cultural Dictionary.* London: SCM Press, 1996.

Bibliography

Ryken, Leland, et al., eds. *Dictionary of Biblical Imagery*. Downers Grove, IL: InterVarsity Press, 1998.

Sabourin, Léopold. *Il Vangelo di Matteo: Teologia e esegesi. Nuova edizione aumentata*. Vol. 1. Rome: Edizioni Paolini, 1976.

Sacks, Rabbi Jonathan. *Not in God's Name: Confronting Religious Violence*. New York: Schocken, 2017.

Safrai, Shmuel, et al., eds. *The Literature of the Sages*. Compendia rerum Iudaicarum ad Novum Testamentum 3, second part. Assen, Netherlands: Van Gorcum, 1987.

Sawyer, John F.A. *Sacred Languages and Sacred Texts*. London: Routledge, 1999.

Stransky, Thomas. "The Genesis of *Nostra Aetate*." *America*, October 24, 2005.

Tobias, Norman. "Jules Isaac and the Roman Catholic Church: Advocate for Scriptural Truth." PhD diss., University of Toronto, 2015.

Torrance, Thomas F. *Atonement: The Person and Work of Christ*. Downers Grove, IL: InterVarsity Press, 2014.

Toynbee, Arnold J. *A Study of History*. London: Oxford University Press, 1987.

Tuttle, Gary A., ed. *Biblical and Near Eastern Studies: Essays in Honor of William Sanford LaSor*. Grand Rapids: Eerdmans, 1978.

Venuti, Lawrence. *The Translator's Invisibility: A History of Translation*. London: Routledge, 1995.

Vigouroux, F., ed. *Dictionnaire de la Bible*. Vol 4. Paris: Letouzey et Ané, 1912.

Vorgrimler, Herbert, ed. *Commentary on the Documents of Vatican II*. London: Burns & Oates, 1969.

Vriezen, Theodor Christiaan, and A. S. van der Woude. *Ancient Israelite and Early Christian Literature*. 10th rev. ed. Leiden: Brill, 2005.

Willebrands, Johannes G. M. *Church and Jewish People: New Considerations*. Mahwah, NJ: Paulist, 1992.

Wistrich, Robert S., ed. *Terms of Survival: The Jewish World since 1945*. London: Routledge, 1995.

Zorell, Franz. "Maria, soror Mosis et Maria, Mater Dei." *Verbum Domini* 6 (1926).

INDEX

Entries in **bold** denote illustrations.

Adept, 48, 49
Aïn-Témouchent, 85, 87–88
Albanel, Christine, 131
Algeria, 85–88, 93, 98–100, 105–8
Amaryllis, 59, 62–63
Angels, 43–44, **43, 44**
Anti-Semitism, 87–88, 90, 96, 100, 110
Apostleship, 50–52
Aquila, 7
Aslanov, Cyril, 83–84
Assaf, Ami, 115
Augustine, 63–64

Bea, Augustin, 109
Beatitudes, 57–58
Begin, Menachem, 123, 124
Ben-Chorin, Schalom, 15
Benedictus, 30
Ben-Gurion, David, 114, 115–17
ben-Nissim, Jacob, 39
Ben-Zvi, Yitzhak, 114
Berlin, Naftali Avi Yehuah, 154n3
Bethlehem, 34
Between East and West (Chouraqui), 86

Boyer, Colete, 98–102, 104, 110–11, 124–25, 165n102, 165n107
Browne, Lewis, 15
Buber, Martin, 15–18
Bush, George W., 136–37

Camp David Accords, 123–24
Camus, Albert, 102–3
Carlyle, Thomas, 78
Carmignac, Jean, 30
Carter, Jimmy, 124
Chairein/chérir, 163n78
Chilton, Bruce D., 6, 41–42
Chouraqui, Isaac, 85–86
Chouraqui, André: Abrahamic faiths, 127, 134–35, 137, 142; advisor, Ben-Gurion, 115–17; Algeria, 85–88, 93, 98–100, 105–8; *aliyah*, 112, 113–17; angels, 44; apostleship, 51–52; autobiographies, 84–85, 88, 103, 124, 126, 127; Beatitudes, 57–58; and Ben-Gurion, 114, 115–16; biblical circles, 116–17; books, 86, 88, 103, 112–13, 121, 124–25, 126, 127–28; and Boyer, 98–102, 104,

177

110–11, 124–25, 165n102, 165n107; and Camus, 102–3; and Christ, 19–20, 22, 23, 24–25, 34, 43, 53–54, 138, 140–42; and Christianity, 13–14, 89, 95–96, 103–4, 132–33; cognates, 70, 73; death, 128, 132, 136; deputy mayor, 118; dialogue, 4, 85, 120–21, 137; discipleship, 47–48; dynamic equivalence, 25; education, 90–96, 115; etymology, 21, 34, 47, 139; French Legion of Honor, 126–27; French Resistance, 102–4; Gospels, 22–23; historical accuracy, 35; and Isaac, 109, 137; and Islam, 88–89, 120, 125, 126, 136–37; Israel, 111–12, 113–14; Jerusalem, 68–69, 111–12, 114–15, 117–19, 127; and Judaism, 13–14, 91–93, 96–97, 132–33, 138, 140–42; and Kollek, 118; language, 87, 138, 139–40; legal studies, 95, 97; and Levy, 114; life, 83–135; marriage, 99–100; Mary, 28; names, 25–30, 85–86; New Testament, 8; place names, 31–35; political career, 8–9, 115–21, 123–24; priesthood, vocabulary, 37–38; prophecy, 45–47; Qur'an, translation of, 125, 126; rabbi, vocabulary, 38–43; rabbinic studies, 96–97; religious observance, 91–93; Renaissance man, 134–35; reunification of Jerusalem, 117–19; and Scripture, 14, 22, 93–95, 97, 116; and Second Vatican Council, 109, 117–18; Semitic voice of Bible, 22; Sorbonne, 94–95; spirit, 52–53; surgery, 93; *teshuvah*, 96; translation, 5, 9–10, 13, 22–23, 25, 77–78, 113, 121–23, 125–26, 129–32, 138–40; tributes, 128–32; vocabulary, 36; war, 98–105

Chouraqui Bible. See *La Bible Chouraqui*

Christianity: Algeria, 87–88; and Chouraqui, 13–14, 89, 95–96, 103–4; and Judaism, 13–14, 23, 79–80, 87–89, 101–2, 132–34; and Nazi persecution of Jews, 101–2

Chronique de Baba (Chouraqui), 127

Clermont-Ferrand, 101

Cognates, 69–73

Cohen, Shaye J. D., 40

Comité pour l'Entente religieuse en Israël et dans le monde, 114

Cotton Batch Gospels, 138

de Bourqueney, Jean-Marie, 59

Deliztsch, Franz, 161n50

Deschanel, Jacques, 122

Desservant, 38

Index

Dialogue: Buber, 17; Chouraqui, 4, 85, 137; interreligious, 4, 23, 85, 120–21, 133–34, 137; translation, 17
Didaskalos, 39, 40, 42–43
Discipleship, 47–49
Discipulis, 47
Duling, Dennis C., 50

Egypt, 31
Elihai, Yahanan, 131–32
Elijah, 29–30
Elohim, 66
Envoy, 51–52
Etymology, 21, 26, 34, 47, 139

Felici, Pericle, 117
Ferguson, Everett, 49–50
Finkelstein, Bluma, 133–34
Flesher, Paul V. M., 6
Flusser, David, 15
Fox, Everett, 18–19, 157n18
France, 94–95, 98–99, 126–27
Fraternité d'Abraham, 120
Frye, Northrop, 25

Galilee, 31–32
Gevaryahu, Haim, 116
Gibbs, Robert, 17
Gill, John, 54–55
Ginsburg, David, 161n50
God, name of, 164n79
Good as New translation, 138
Gospels: Chouraqui, 22–23; cognates, 70–73; discipleship, 48–49; and Judaism, 23; priesthood, 36–37; rabbis, 38–40; Semitic/Hebrew, 30–31, 158n28; translation, 22–23. *See also* Jesus Christ; New Testament
Grace, 29
"Great men," 78–79
Greek language, 5, 6–7, 21–22, 28–30, 35, 54, 69–70, 74

Hassan II, King, 123
Hebrew Bible: dual/plural endings, 31, 65–66; etymology, 26; and Greek, 70, 74; imperfect tense, 73; translation, 5–7
Hebrew language, 5–6
Hebrews, Epistle to, 67–68
Henry, Patrick, 102–3
Herzl, Theodor, 79
Hexapla, 154n5
Holocaust. *See* Shoah
Holy Spirit, 52–53
Hosanna, 27
Hutter, Elias, 160n50

ibn Paquda, Baḥya, 112–13
Inspired one, 45–47
Integration of Ethnic Communities, 115
Isaac, Jules, 109, 137
Islam, 88–89, 120, 125, 126, 136–37
Israel, 79–80, 111–12, 115

James, Apostle, 29
Jerome, 63–64
Jerusalem, 66–68, 111–12, 114–15, 117–19, 127, 163n76

Jesus Christ: and Chouraqui, 19–20, 22, 23, 24–25, 34, 43, 53–54, 138, 140–42; discipleship, 48–49; garments, 54–56, **56;** INRI, 156n13, and Judaism, 14–15, 19–23, 34, 53–54, 138, 140–42; name, 25–26; and Nazareth, 33; rabbi, 43; salvation, 27; Semitic voice, 22
John Paul II, Pope, 20, 124, 125–26
John the Baptist, 28–29, 42
John XXIII, Pope, 109, 117, 167n130
Judaism: Algeria, 86, 87–88; Bible translation, 4, 6, 7–8, 15–17; and Christ, 14–15, 23, 34, 53–54, 138, 140–42; and Chouraqui, 13–14, 91–93, 96–97, 132–33, 138, 140–42; Christianity, 13–14, 23, 79–80, 87–89, 101–2, 132–34; Clermont-Ferrand, 101; and Gospels, 23; and Islam, 88–89; and Nazis, 100–102; New Testament, 7–8, 13–15, 134; North Africa, 86, 91; rabbis, 39–42; Second Temple, 14–15. *See also* Anti-Semitism

Katsir, Ephraim, 123
Kaufmann, Francine, 84
Kollek, Teddy, 118
Krašovec, Jože, 26
Krinon, 59–62

La Bible Chouraqui: goals, 4–5, 142; iconoclastic, 77–78; Jewish, 4; John the Baptist, 28–29; methods and intent, 5; and other translations, 19; output, 10; process, 10, 121–23; publication, 10; reactions, 4, 129–32
L'amour fort comme la mort (Chouraqui), 103, 126
Language: Chouraqui, 87, 138, 139–40; English, 3; French, 4; future tense, 73–76; Greek, 5, 6–7, 21–22, 28–30, 35, 54, 69–70, 74; healing, interfaith, 142; Hebrew, 5–6; imperfect tense, 73; meaning, 7; Tower of Babel, 141; translation, 3–7
La reconnaisance (Chouraqui), 126
Latroun, 10
Le destin d'Israël, 128
Leiva-Merikakis, Erasmo, 58–59
Les Amis d'André Chouraqui, 136
Les Misérables, 69
Lettre à un ami arabe (Chouraqui), 120
Levy, Annette, 114
Liber, Maurice, 97
Lilies of the field, 59–62
Little Sisters of Jesus, 110
Lottman, Herbert, 102
L'Univers de la Bible (Chouraqui), 124–25, 139
Luther, Martin, 15–16

Index

Magdala, 32
Man in Three Worlds, A (Chouraqui), 88, 124
Mark, Gospel of, 69–70. *See also* Gospels
Mary, 25, 28
Meier, John, 21
Merino, Luis, Díez, 28
Messiah, the, 41, 79, 154n3, 159n39
Meyer, Abraham (Baba), 87, 88, 127
Meyer, Meléha, 85
Mitterand, François, 126–27
Mon testament (Chouraqui), 127
Morselli, Marco, 154n3
Mystery religions, 48–50

Names, 25–35
Navon, Yitzhak, 124
Nazareth, 33
Naziism, 16, 17, 98, 100–102
New Testament: Chouraqui, 8; Judaism, 7–8, 13–15, 134; translation, 7–8, 134
9/11, 136, 137
Nostra aetate, 109–10, 117, 167n130

Opus sacerdotale Amici Israel, 80
Ossuaries, 40

Paul, Apostle, 67
Paul VI, Pope, 123, 167n130
Peres, Shimon, 219
Perrin, Norman, 50
Peter, Apostle, 29

Pius X, Pope, 79–80, 109
Pontifex, 37–38
Presbyteros, 37
Priesthood, 36–38
Prophecy, 45–53

Qiqayon, 63–64

Rabbis, 38–43
Ridderbos, Herman N., 39
Rosenzweig, Franz, 15–18
Rouche, Rabbi, 99
Rousseau, John J., 32

Sacks, Jonathan, 154n3
Sacred breath, 53
Sadat, Anwar, 123
Salkinson, Isaac, 161n50
Salvation, 27
Samaria, 32–33
Sarkozy, Nicolas, 128–29
Sawyer, John F. A., 25
Scripture: biblical circles, Ben-Gurion, 116–17; Chouraqui, 10, 14, 22, 93–95, 97, 116; Semitic voice, 22; translation, 5, 9–10, 13, 22–23. *See also* Hebrew Bible; New Testament; Translation; Vocabulary
Second Vatican Council, 109, 117
Septuagint, 155nn4–5
Shanks, Hershel, 40
Shoah, 8, 100–101, 103, 153n1
Spinoza, Baruch, 94
Spirit, 46–47, 52–53
Sukenik, Eleazar, 40

Talmud, 97
Targums, 6
Tense, verb. *See under* Language
Tincq, Henri, 129–31
Ton étoile et la crois (Chouraqui), 127
Torrance, Thomas F., 51
Tower of Babel, 3, 141, 154n3
Translation: Buber and Rosenzweig, 15–18; Chouraqui, 5, 8, 25, 77–78, 113, 121–23, 125–26, 129–32, 138–40; dialogue, 17; dynamic equivalence, 11–12; English, 3; formal equivalence, 12, 25; Fox, 18–19; French, 4, 77; German, 15–16; goals, 4–5; Gospels, 22–23; Hebrew Bible, 5–7; Jewish, 4, 6, 7–8, 15–17; literal, 12; New Testament, 7–8; Qur'an, 125, 126; theory, 11–12
Tzitzit, 54–57, **56, 57**

Ubaldine, Sister, 89

van er Woude, A. S., 45
Venuti, Lawrence, 11, 12
Vermes, Geza, 15
Vichy government, 100
Vivre pour Jérusalem (Chouraqui), 121
Vocabulary, biblical: angels, 43–44; priesthood, 36–38; prophecy, 45–53; rabbis, 38–44
Vriezen, Christiaan, 45

World War II, 98–105

Yerushalayim. *See* Jerusalem
Yohanan, Rabbi, 67

Zeitlin, Solomon, 40
Zorell, Franz, 28

OTHER VOLUMES IN THIS SERIES

Clemens Thoma and Michael Wyschogrod, eds., *Understanding Scripture: Explorations of Jewish and Christian Traditions of Interpretation* (1987; e-book only)

Bernard J. Lee, *The Galilean Jewishness of Jesus: Retrieving the Origins of Christianity (Conversation on the Road Not Taken, Vol. I)* (1988; e-book only)

Clemens Thoma and Michael Wyschogrod, eds., *Parable and Story in Judaism and Christianity* (1989)

Eugene J. Fisher, ed., *Interwoven Destinies: Jews and Christians through the Ages* (1992; e-book only)

George M. Smiga, *Pain and Polemic: Anti-Judaism in the Gospels* (1992; e-book only)

Anthony J. Kenny, *Catholics, Jews, and the State of Israel* (1993; e-book only)

Eugene J. Fisher, ed., *Visions of the Other: Jewish and Christian Theologians Assess the Dialogue* (1994; e-book only)

Vincent Martin, *A House Divided: The Parting of the Ways between Synagogue and Church* (1995; e-book only)

Leon Klenicki and Geoffrey Wigoder, *A Dictionary of the Jewish-Christian Dialogue* (1995; e-book only)

Frank E. Eakin Jr., *What Price Prejudice? Christian Antisemitism in America* (1998)

Philip A. Cunningham and Arthur F. Starr, eds., *Sharing Shalom: A Process for Local Interfaith Dialogue between Christians and Jews* (1999)

Ekkehard Schuster and Reinhold Boschert-Kimmig, *Hope against Hope: Johann Baptist Metz and Elie Wiesel Speak Out on the Holocaust* (1999)

Mary C. Boys, *Has God Only One Blessing? Judaism as a Source of Christian Self-Understanding* (2000)

Johannes Reuchlin; translated and edited by Peter Wortsman, *Recommendation Whether to Confiscate, Destroy and Burn All Jewish Books: A Classic Treatise against Anti-Semitism* (2000)

Avery Dulles and Leon Klenicki, *The Holocaust, Never to Be Forgotten: Reflections on the Holy See's Document* We Remember (2001)

OTHER VOLUMES IN THIS SERIES

Philip A. Cunningham, *A Story of Shalom: the Calling of Christians and Jews by a Covenanting God* (2001; e-book only)

Philip A. Cunningham, *Sharing the Scriptures: The Word Set Free, Volume 1* (2003)

Dina Wardi, *Auschwitz: Contemporary Jewish and Christian Encounters* (2003)

Michael Lotker, *A Christian's Guide to Judaism* (2004)

Edward H. Flannery, *The Anguish of the Jews: Twenty-Three Centuries of Antisemitism (Revised and Updated)* (2004)

Lawrence Boadt, CSP, and Kevin di Camillo, eds., *John Paul II in the Holy Land: In His Own Words; With Christian and Jewish Perspectives by Yehezkel Landau and Michael McGarry, CSP* (2005)

James K. Aitken and Edward Kessler, eds., *Challenges in Jewish-Christian Relations* (2006)

Steven C. Boguslawski, OP, *Thomas Aquinas on the Jews: Insights into His Commentary on Romans 9–11* (2008)

George M. Smiga, *The Gospel of John Set Free: Preaching without Anti-Judaism* (2008)

Daniel J. Harrington, SJ, *The Synoptic Gospels Set Free: Preaching without Anti-Judaism* (2009)

Richard C. Lux, *The Jewish People, the Holy Land, and the State of Israel: A Catholic View* (2009)

Cardinal Jean-Marie Lustiger, edited by Jean Duchesne, *Cardinal Jean-Marie Lustiger on Christians and Jews* (2010)

Pope Benedict XVI, *Pope Benedict XVI in the Holy Land* (2010)

Thomas G. Casey and Justin Taylor, eds., *Paul's Jewish Matrix* (2011)

Franklin Sherman, ed., *Bridges—Documents of the Christian-Jewish Dialogue: Volume One—The Road to Reconciliation (1945–1985)* (2011)

Eugene J. Fisher, eds., Memoria Futuri: *Catholic-Jewish Dialogue Yesterday, Today, and Tomorrow; Texts and Addresses of Cardinal William H. Keeler* (2012)

Mary C. Boys, *Redeeming Our Sacred Story: The Death of Jesus and Relations between Jews and Christians* (2013)

OTHER VOLUMES IN THIS SERIES

Celia M. Deutsch, Eugene J. Fisher, and James Rudin, eds., *Toward the Future: Essays on Catholic-Jewish Relations in Memory of Rabbi León Klenicki* (2013)

Franklin Sherman, ed., *Bridges—Documents of the Christian-Jewish Dialogue: Volume Two—Building a New Relationship (1986–2013)* (2014)

Ronald Kronish, ed., *Coexistence and Reconciliation in Israel: Voices for Interreligious Dialogue* (2015)

Elena G. Procario-Foley and Robert A. Cathey, eds., *Righting Relations after the Holocaust and Vatican II: Essays in Honor of John Pawlikowski, OSM* (2018)

Paula Fredriksen and Jesper Svartvik, eds., *Krister among the Jews and Gentiles* (2018)

Carol Rittner, Stephen D. Smith, and Irena Steinfeldt. *The Holocaust and the Christian World: Reflections on the Past, Challenges for the Future*, 2nd Edition (2019)

Philip A. Cunningham, Ruth Langer, and Jesper Svartvik, eds., *Enabling Dialogue about the Land: A Resource Book for Jews and Christians* (2020)

Philip A. Cunningham, *Maxims for Mutuality: Principles for Catholic Theology, Education, and Preaching about Jews and Judaism* (2022)

Teresa Pirola, *Catholic-Jewish Relations: Twelve Key Themes for Teaching & Preaching* (2023)

STIMULUS BOOKS are developed by the Stimulus Foundation, a not-for-profit organization, and are published by Paulist Press. The Foundation wishes to further the publication of scholarly books on Jewish and Christian topics that are of importance to Judaism and Christianity.

The Stimulus Foundation was established by an erstwhile refugee from Nazi Germany who intends to contribute with these publications to the improvement of communication between Jews and Christians.

Books for publication in this Series will be selected by a committee of the Foundation, and offers of manuscripts and works in progress should be addressed to:

The Stimulus Foundation
c/o Paulist Press
997 Macarthur Boulevard
Mahwah, NJ 07430
www.paulistpress.com